Thirty Years o

Thirty Years of Honesty

Honest to God Then and Now

Edited by John Bowden

SCM PRESS LTD

0 334 02362 9

First published 1993
by SCM Press Ltd
26–30 Tottenham Road, London N1 4BZ

Phototypeset by Selwood Systems, Midsomer Norton
and printed in Great Britain by
Biddles Ltd, Guildford and King's Lynn

Contents

II *Honest to God* Now

Editor's Preface

Those who have never seen a copy should know that John A. T. Robinson's *Honest to God* is a small-format paperback of 144 pages, first published by SCM Press in March 1963. It is still in print, the twenty-second impression being dated 1991, and has on its cover an illustration of Wilhelm Lehmbruck's 'Seated Youth'. *The Guardian* once called it 'probably the most talked-about theological work of this century' and 'Seated Youth' virtually became a logo in its own right.

This commemoration, thirty years after, arose out of five talks on BBC Radio Four in the series 'Seeds of Faith'. The series was the brainchild of the producer Norman Winter, and we are grateful to him, his colleagues and the British Broadcasting Corporation for making its publication possible. Because five half-hour broadcasts do not in themselves make a book, we decided to supplement them with some of the original 1963 responses, and David Edwards, Editor and Managing Director of SCM Press at the time of the publication of *Honest to God*, has kindly written an Introduction specially for the volume.

The invitations to those who gave the BBC talks also requested suggestions for appropriate music – not an easy task, since a love of music was certainly not among John Robinson's fortes! It was of course impossible to include that dimension here, but the request may explain some references in the text – and those who know the passages concerned may like to imagine them in the background at appropriate points. Speakers were also asked to include quotations, to be read by a different voice; these we have included where possible, and are grateful to the copyright holders for permission to include them: due acknowledgments are given elsewhere.

The commemoration speaks for itself and needs no further

comment from me. However, perhaps just one thing should be said about the title of John Robinson's book, the brilliant suggestion of his wife. I know of only one other recent title which has proved to have quite the power, for better or worse, than *Honest to God*, and that is Salman Rushdie's *The Satanic Verses*. In each case the title has gone on to lead a life of its own, provoking tremendous reactions from people who have never read or even seen the book. And in each case the title has become a complex symbol, suggesting more than the author could ever have dreamed of.

That is why the *Honest to God* phenomenon is still worth thinking about and reflecting on, and has gone down as a landmark in the history of English Christianity.

John Bowden

July 1993

Introduction

David L. Edwards

Thirty years ago I was glad and proud to be the publisher of John Robinson's *Honest to God.* I still am. And to be honest, one of my reasons was, and is, that it was a best-seller. I boasted that its million copies in many languages constituted the quickest sale of any book of serious theology in the history of the world. And this sensation of the 1960s has gone on being read and thought about.

Young people looking round for a career both enjoyable and profitable are often told that 'you can't go into publishing as a Managing Director'. Well, I did – and I had a wonderful eight years,based in an office near the British Museum. Publishing is so attractive because one is dealing with ideas or imaginations and helping to create beauty, or at least good order, in words and design; yet one is also in a commercial firm, having the stimulus of competing with others to get tangible results and the excitement that every new book is a gamble – but also having the support of a team of colleagues with the same motivation. A lot of it is humdrum, of course; it is not all lunches or publicity. During my time there the SCM Press published many books which reached an appreciative but quite small public – books of biblical or theological scholarship (often translated laboriously) and more popular books about issues in church life or in the life of the individual Christian. But it was nice to be a midwife at the birth of a book which was both bought and discussed by a very large number of deeply interested readers. Because of it, the Ground of Being was temporarily a topic for conversation in pubs.

I had conceived the ambition of producing a series of paperbacks which looked like the Pelican books then plentifully published by Penguin and were not much more expensive. One of the many changes of the 1960s was the paperback revolution in the bookshops. Some serious non-fiction could be sold and bought like a novel, although in England the time had not yet come when big books could appear decently in their first editions without cloth covers. I invited John Robinson, a New Testament scholar and a new bishop, to contribute to this series and he felt able to accept because back trouble meant that he had some months free to think about his own religious position instead of attending to academic or pastoral duties. When the draft of his typescript arrived, I saw that it would arouse some controversy because here was a bishop speaking in a personal way about ideas which were familiar to me and to some in my circle but not to the public. However, I did not get very excited and we printed only eight thousand copies, two thousand of those being for an American publisher. In this book Eric James, John Robinson's biographer, records what followed.

I am still delighted about the profit which the firm made by selling *Honest to God*, the books we had brought out earlier and which it recommended, and the books which followed by way of sequel or response. That was one of the foundations of the brilliant achievement of my successor, John Bowden, in the translation and selling of theology over a quarter of a century. I do not know why he sounds so depressed in his broadcast printed in this book. Of course not enough people are interested in theology – no one who tries to write or recommend it will dispute that! But as the leading publisher in this field in the English-speaking world, John Bowden has built a temple to the God who is Truth, with hundreds of books of solid value. A sufficient public has paid for that and some of it must have come from the churches, although many of the grateful readers are no doubt at least semi-detached from any ecclesiastical structure. In the Church of England (a comparatively small outfit), successive reports of the Doctrine Commission have been far from bigoted. Archbishop Michael Ramsey lived to regret his initial indifference or hostility to *Honest to God*; he told me and others so more than once. When John Robinson died

Archbishop Robert Runcie secured his personal library of theology for Lambeth Palace. Among recent publications by the SCM Press which seem to me both honest and constructive is *The Christlike God* by John Taylor, formerly Bishop of Winchester. Most regular churchgoers, in England or any other country, are of course conservative in that they have grown to love what has become familiar; in that tradition they have found comfort and joy. And most church leaders are more sensitive towards their flocks than towards any sheep which do not want to know them. But in the second half of the twentieth century the changes accepted in the churches have been as great as they were during the Reformation and Counter-Reformation of the sixteenth century. The most dramatic novelties have been the renewal of Roman Catholicism unleashed by the Second Vatican Council and the spread of the Pentecostal or Charismatic movement like wind or fire, but almost every church building in the world has been the scene of changes and almost everywhere part of the new mood has been a concentration on the centre of Christianity as this centre is (rightly or wrongly) felt to be strong by personal experience and reflection. Contrast the failures of political movements in the period! Or contrast the unintelligibility of high culture in the age of television!

It has been a very confusing period, for Christians no less than for the world as a whole. When I edited *The Honest to God Debate*, a paperback of almost 300 pages published in the autumn of 1963 to reflect the controversy, I contributed an introduction celebrating 'A New Stirring in English Christianity'. Already in 1963 there had been many changes in the English churches, as elsewhere around the world. Instead of the tired repetition of dogmas, there was a new interest in the dramas of life and thought in the Bible – an interest formalized (and over-organized) at the academic level in 'biblical theology' but also building up into the movements (Catholic or Evangelical) which were to put new translations of the Bible into the hands and hearts of millions. The worship in the churches was beginning to be renewed – a renewal which was to lead to the arrival of a flood of new prayers and hymns and to the marginalization of Latin, Tudor English and similar echoes of a vanished world, with the physical transformation of many churches to make the worship more corporate. The ecumenical movement was beginning to gather force – a change which was to alter for many (not for all) the whole way in which Christians adhering to still divided churches look at one another. The application of Christianity to society's problems was also quite vigorous, and was to develop into a new attitude to sex, into Christian feminism, into the spiritual victory over Communism and into the 'liberation theology' which has made the Christians more prophetic and even influential than the Communists in much of the Two-Thirds World. But I also celebrated the beginning of a renewal of doctrine and belief, coming to a head in England with the controversy about *Honest to God* but also already widespread elsewhere. I observed of course that this was proving to be the most difficult part of the necessary renewal. Here the questions are the hardest which can be asked and the answers are hotly contested because (to use Tillich's phrases which Robinson popularized) they spring out of 'ultimate concern' for 'ultimate reality'.

In my own journey since 1963 I have not been entirely sheltered from the storms. It is true that I have loved and served some great churches: St Martins-in-the-Fields in Trafalgar Square, King's College Chapel in Cambridge, Westminster Abbey and St Margaret's next to it, Norwich Cathedral in peaceful Norfolk, Southwark Cathedral back in London. But like many clergy in the period I have felt keenly the difficulty of persuading most people that they might find at least part of what they are looking for in church. I have felt that when surrounded by the crowds in central London, by university students, by the House of Commons to whose speaker I was Chaplain, by Norfolk people, by inner-city people or office workers in South London. And if I may continue to be personal for a bit longer, I have been immersed in the confusion of our religious situation as I have written my own books. These have not only been history books about the heritage which retains my allegiance. They have included one dialogue with an Evangelical leader more conservative than I am and another with radical theologians more unorthodox than I am. I have written a response (which may be thought heretical) to the new *Catechism of the Catholic Church*. And in other books I have tackled problems in reading the Old and New Testaments. Moreover, I have felt many disturbances in my own life and faith.

I mention these experiences in order to claim some qualifications for saying that as the debate about the issues raised by *Honest to God* has continued it has become obvious that two very different trends have emerged which were brought together in John Robinson's paperback, at least to some extent. This explains why so many readers were stirred by that book, but stirred in different ways. Some were shocked that this scholarly bishop had been so influenced by contemporaries whose thought was more secular, more superficial and more muddled than the truths which shone in his own tradition; and they urged him to return home. Up to a point, Robinson eventually showed that he agreed with the reaction, for he moved back to Cambridge university, he concentrated on defending the historical reliability of the New Testament, and when he came to die he drew courage and strength from the psalms and from other ancient sources of faith. But other readers of *Honest to God* wished that he would see the logic of his position – a logic which to them meant atheism, or at least a religion far wider than Christianity, or at least a revision of Christianity which would leave few landmarks standing. And up to a point, Robinson agreed with this reaction too. He studied and expounded the literature of a mysticism which was not communion with the 'personal' God, he became very interested in Indian religion, he continued to be an *enfant terrible* among bishops – which explains why he was never offered another ecclesiastical post. In this book his widow, to whom I think he was always devoted, contributes a chapter which powerfully reflects this half of John Robinson. In the light of his later life, it is understandable that when *Honest to God* was fresh people told each other not to judge it without reading it – and then after such study as they managed, disagreed vehemently about what it meant. Was he a revolutionary, however 'reluctant'? And what revolution did he want?

I need not add to the analysis of problems raised by the text of *Honest to God* which I offered in my own book on *Tradition and Truth* (1989). But here I may draw attention to the divergence within the contents of this book. The reader will find a reprint of part of an essay in which a theologian lamented with some passion that 'the Bishop' (a significant way of referring to Robinson) had not done justice to the great tradition in which Christians had been grasped by the mystery of the living, active God. (That theologian was David Jenkins, who went on to become the Bishop of Durham who has been accused of all manner of heresies.) The reader will also find another theologian, Ruth Etchells, lamenting in a recent broadcast that *Honest to God* found no room for the mystery of the resurrection of Jesus, where the living God acted to confirm the human hope of heaven. But in a reprint of a 1963 review yet another theologian, Alec Graham, who was to become Bishop of Newcastle and Chairman of the Church of England's Doctrine Commission, usually classified as a learned conservative, demonstrates that *Honest to God* was essentially within the orthodox Christian tradition. On the other hand, in addition to the articles by John Bowden and Ruth Robinson which imply that *Honest to God* did not move far enough to the Christian left, we are given a broadcast by Alan Race which implies that when John Robinson visited India geographically and spiritually he did not go far enough into the proper disclaimer of Christianity's superiority to other religions. And there is a reference to Don Cupitt, John Robinson's successor as the most controversial Cambridge theologian – and one who had friendly arguments with Robinson. Cupitt moved into the conviction that God and eternal life, although symbols of enduring value, are themselves unreal. Indeed, we are told that some young clergy share this conviction (conventionally termed atheism) but have to keep quiet about it in a church which has become more or less fundamentalist. With due respect, I have to ask whether such clergy provide a model of honesty.

So the debate continues. It was outspoken within John Robinson's mind and in his writing which was more turbulently and provocatively eloquent than lucid: he had a gift for piercing phrases more than for a dull balance. The debate will be stirred into new life in the mind of any reader who ponders this book. My own hope is that in the end polarization will be overcome and the discussion will settle down into a general (it could never be a unanimous) consensus on a few vital points. I hope for agreement that the mystery which in the English language is indicated by the three letters G, O and D is worth exploring, although in the end the exploration will cost 'not less than everything'. It is a mystery which most people enter through the experience of human love; that was why John Robinson, the author of *Exploration into God*, was able to reach *Daily Mirror* readers in the article reprinted here. But a reality of love beyond the human is also glimpsed. That is what the great religions of humanity are ultimately about. Each of these religions is a path into the mystery, and surely we should need many eyes to see the whole truth. But Jesus is unique and (yes!) superior to other prophets because in his human life the love which God has for us can be found embodied for our salvation. And the Christian church is not going to die, because, for all its limitations, errors and sins, it puts that continuing life within our reach. This 'Beyond' is, however, glimpsed only if the moments of intuition which probably come to all human beings are interpreted with faith, faith meaning trust as in a happy marriage, going beyond our certain knowledge although not against it.

In Southwark Cathedral, a memorial to John Robinson is appropriate because when he wrote *Honest to God* he was a bishop in our diocese. It is a sculpture in wood by his brother, Edward. It invites the onlooker to become involved by opening doors which on the outside are rugged and black. Inside the pattern on the doors is repeated but in light wood and white paint. We call the sculpture Resurrection.

I

Honest to God Then

Why I Wrote It

John A. T. Robinson

Some years ago Mr Gaitskell proposed revising the famous Clause Four of the Labour Party's constitution (on nationalization).

Those who opposed him dubbed it all 'theology' – theoretical statements about things that make no practical difference.

Such is the name that 'theology' has gained. But suddenly that image seems to have changed.

Up till now the Press took notice of clergymen only if they spoke on morals or politics. What they said on God and the Gospel was ignored. Archbishop William Temple constantly complained of this. But now 'God' is news!

My book seems to have touched people at a point where truth really matters to them. And of that I am glad – even if it has meant some pain.

For God is to be found at the point where things really do matter to us.

What drove me to write my book was that this is simply not true for most people.

What matters to them most in life seems to have nothing to do with 'God'; and God has no connection with what really concerns them day by day.

At best he seems to come in only at the edge of life. He is out there somewhere as a sort of long-stop – at death, or to turn to in tragedy (either to pray to or to blame).

The traditional imagery of God simply succeeds, I believe, in making him remote for millions today.

What I want to do is not to deny God in any sense, but to

put him back into the middle of life – where Jesus showed us he belongs.

For the Christian God is not remote. He is involved; he is implicated. If Jesus Christ means anything, he means that God belongs to this world.

So let's start not from a heavenly Being, whose very existence many would doubt. Let's start from what actually is most real to people in everyday life – and find God there.

What is most real to you? What matters most for you? Is it money, and what money can buy?

I doubt it, deep down. For you know that you 'can't take it with you'. And seldom does it bring real happiness.

Is it love? That's a good deal nearer, because it has to do with persons, not things.

But what is love? Sex? Sex is a marvellous part of it. But sex by itself can leave people deeply unsatisfied. Remember Marilyn Monroe?

We all need, more than anything else, to love and be loved. That's what the psychologists tell us. But by that they mean we need to be *accepted* as persons, as whole persons, for our own sake.

And this is what true love does. It accepts people, without any strings, simply for what they are. It gives them worth. It 'makes their lives'.

That is precisely what we see Jesus doing in the Gospels, making and re-making people's lives, bringing meaning back to them.

In him we see love at work, in a way that the world has never seen before or since.

And that's why the New Testament sees God at work in him – for God is love. In the Cross that love comes out to the uttermost. 'There's love for you!' says Calvary.

And in the Resurrection we see that not even death was able to destroy its power to transform and heal. Love still came out top.

The Christian is the one who believes in *that* love as the last word for life.

It is quite simply the ultimate reality: it is God.

The universe, like a human being, is not built merely to a mathematical formula. It's only love that gives you the deepest clue to it.

'It's love that makes the world go round.' That's what all Christians have always said. But so often they have *pictured* it in a way that makes it difficult for modern men and women to see it.

They have spoken as though what makes the world go round were an old man in the sky, a supernatural Person.

Of course, they don't take that literally. It helps only to make God easier to *imagine*. But it can also hinder.

Perhaps a comparison will show what I mean.

The ancient Greeks thought of the earth being upheld on the shoulders of a superman called Atlas. That was their way of saying that it doesn't support itself in space.

We also know that it doesn't. For us it is held in orbit by the sun's gravitational pull.

The ancient myth was saying something true. But such language today would not convey the truth to us. It would be much more likely to conceal it.

So with Christian truth. The reality is that in Jesus we see the clue to all life. To say that he was the Son of a supernatural Being sent to earth from heaven may help to bring this home.

But for others it may take it out of their world altogether – so that the events of Christmas and Holy Week seem to belong to a religious fairy story.

If the traditional way of putting it makes Christ real for you – the most real thing in the world – well and good. I don't want to destroy anyone's imagery of God.

I wrote my book for those who have increasingly come to feel that it makes him unreal and remote.

I tried to be honest about what God means to me – in the second half of the twentieth century.

The hundreds of letters I have received, particularly from the younger generation, inside the church and out of it, have convinced me that I may have rung a bell for others too.

For that I can only be humbly thankful.

For I want God to be as real for our modern secular, scientific world as he ever was for the 'ages of faith'.

First published in the *Sunday Mirror* of 7 April 1963 and reprinted in *The Honest to God Debate*, SCM Press 1963.

The Debate Continues

John A. T. Robinson

The situation could be described by saying that we live in the midst – or at any rate at the beginning – of a currency crisis. It is one that affects all the traditionally accepted means of exchange among Christians and between Christians and the world in which they live: doctrinal formulations, moral codes, liturgical forms, and the rest. These are, as it were, the paper money with which the business of communication is regularly conducted. They are backed in the last resort by certain commitments, certain 'promises of pay', of which they are the token and expression.

Thus, all credal statements, all doctrines, are explications, definitions in the intellectual field, of the commitment contained in the world 'I believe in'. They describe not truths in themselves out of the context of any personal response, but a relationship-in-trust to the various aspects of the truth as it is in Jesus. They say, in greater detail or in less: 'This, when you spell it out, is what is involved in *loving* God with all your *mind*'. Similarly, moral rules, patterns of worship, forms of church order, and the whole Christian style of life, are in the final analysis definitions, declensions of the Christian's commitment-in-love to God and neighbour with all his heart and soul and strength.

To stress this existential, experiential element behind all the Christian's affirmations is not in the least to say that they are purely subjective, in the sense that they represent merely his way of looking at things, his resolve to think or live in a certain manner. The 'promise to pay' is a two-way process. They are expressions of trust in a Reality which is trust-worthy; and the clauses of the Creed, the doctrines and forms of the church, *describe this Reality, not just the individual's inner state*. But they *are* subjective in the sense in which Kierkegaard said that 'Truth is subjectivity'. For truth beyond the level of mere information cannot, he insisted, be apprehended in a purely objective, 'spectator' relationship, but only as a man is prepared to stand, as subject, in an I-Thou relationship of engagement, trust and commitment. It is in this sense that Tillich can say (in his *Systematic Theology* vol. 1, 1953, p. 299), that 'all theological statements are existential': they have all in the last resort to be referred back to this relationship, and their cash value tested by it.

In times of economic stability we do not give thought to what lies behind our paper money: we take it at its face value and use it as a ready and acceptable means of communication and exchange. So in the field of theology: we make statements about God, we issue pronouncements about morals, we set our liturgical commissions to work, we take part in debates on church order and the rest, on the assumption that there is an area of exchange within which these symbols are accepted and valid. And, of course, there is. But in our generation people are increasingly beginning to question whether in fact they *mean anything* or stand for anything real. They ask for their backing, for their cash value.

Within the sterling area, so to speak, the currency holds its own. For those for whom it means business and buys goods there is nothing whatever the matter with it, even though its purchasing power may not be as great as it was in the 'ages of faith', before, as it were, we went off the gold-standard. But the trouble is that the area of convertibility is becoming dangerously restricted: it is increasingly confined to the circle of a religious in-group. The uneasy suspicion is growing that churchpeople may find themselves holding wads of paper money whose exchange value is virtually nil.

There is nothing more unsettling than a currency crisis. It exposes hidden insecurities, it produces panic reactions. And particularly it affects those living on inherited capital or fixed incomes, with nothing new coming in. It is understandable that they should resent anything that appears to weaken confidence still further – even though it may simply be drawing attention to what is happening. And since we all have a far greater stake in the old than we care to admit, no one can treat such a crisis lightly or irresponsibly. It demands endless sympathy, patience and technical skill, to ensure that in the process of revaluation as few as possible get hurt.

Nevertheless, there are two ways of reacting to such a situation. One is to stress the value of the old money at all costs, to strengthen its purchasing power by internal reforms, and to try to extend its area of exchange. The other is to admit that it probably has a limited life and to set about seeing how it can be replaced, while there is time, by other currency, with as little real loss as may be managed.

Both courses may be necessary in the short run if there is not to be a collapse of confidence. And if those carrying responsibility for economic policy in such situations are apt, without loss of integrity, to speak with two voices at once, it is not surprising if responsible theologians and church leaders are to be found doing so too. But what those whom David Edwards describes as 'Christian radicals' are saying is essentially that we should not *fear* the crisis. Indeed, we may actually welcome it, as an opportunity for the church to test on the pulses of experience and commitment what the old paper money is really worth. It is this that accounts for the sense of exhilaration, almost of abandon, that marks some statements of it.

The task with which we are confronted is a double one. First, we must be prepared to ask with rigorous honesty what is the real cash value of the statements we make and the forms we use. We must be ready to be stripped down, and ask how much of the baggage which the Christian church now carries around with it is really necessary, how the doctrines, the liturgies, the systems of morality, the structures and strategies of our church life, are really related to our basic commitment to the grace of our Lord Jesus Christ and the love of God and the fellowship of the Holy Spirit. A currency crisis, if it forces us back on our real assets, can be a salutary shock.

But the second task is that of finding a new currency, that will be convertible in the modern world. And the most distinctive fact about this world is that it is a *secular* world.

I believe that we live in an age in which statements about 'how things are' are expected to have some sort of relationship to people's experience of each other and of things. In other words, theology is not making affirmations about metaphysical realities *per se*, but always describes an experienced relationship or engagement to the truth. It is in this sense that I would agree with Tillich's dictum that 'all theological statements are existential'. They are not objective propositions about 'things in themselves'; but neither are they simply affirmations of my outlook or perspective on life. They are statements about the reality in which my life is grounded as I respond to that reality at the level of 'ultimate concern' (as opposed to proximate concern – the level at which scientific statements, etc., are true).

Perhaps I may illustrate my meaning first with reference to the personality of God in general and then with reference to the doctrine of the Trinity.

The fundamental affirmation which the Christian is making when he says that God is personal is that at its deepest level the reality in which his life is rooted cannot be described exhaustively in terms of impersonal, mathematical regularities but only in the last resort in terms of an utterly gracious and unconditional love, which he can trust as implicitly as at another level he can trust the regularities which science describes. Theological statements are affirmations about the constraint of this love – both as grace and demand – in which the Christian finds himself held. They are descriptions, analyses of the relationship in which he is encountered by reality at this level.

In the past Christians have tended to make many statements which have appeared to characterize a Person in himself rather than a personal relationship. But what lies outside or beyond this relationship we can never say. And if pressed we must be modest and moderate our metaphysical claims. Hitherto we have not been pressed. But the process of secularization, with its distrust of any proposition going beyond the empirical evidence, is forcing the church to strip down its statements and be rigorously honest about what it can claim. In this I believe we have nothing ultimately to lose: indeed, there is a natural reticence in the biblical tradition about 'naming' God or making any pronouncements about him as he is in himself. God is known through his effects. And what theology analyses and describes is the existential relationship in which those effects are known. It is no more speaking of something outside human experience than are comparable analyses of mother-love as an essential constituent of the child's existence as a person. Theology is concerned with the fact that in this relationship of mother-love, as in every other relationship or commitment of life, there are also elements of 'the beyond', claims of the unconditional, which bespeak a depth of reality in which all human love and indeed everything else is grounded. This is the reality which the Christian revelation interprets and defines in terms of the love and grace and fellowship of the Trinity.

The doctrine of the Trinity is not, as it has often been represented, a model of the divine life as it is in itself. It is a formula or definition describing the distinctively Christian encounter with God. Hence all the features in the Trinitarian formula are in the last analysis representations of elements in the existential relationship. For example, the witness of the New Testament and of Christian experience is that it is *in* the Spirit (the medium of the New Being) that we come to the Son and *through* the Son that we come to the Father. Hence, on the 'map' the truth cannot be represented simply by three equidistant points, but only by some way of putting it that includes a progression (the classical doctrine of the 'procession' of the Persons). Nor can the experience be depicted adequately by three relationships to separate 'persons' in the modern sense, each of whom does different things – as, for instance, in the popular theology of the catechism: 'I believe in God the Father, who hath *made* me, and all the world, ... in God the Son, who hath *redeemed* me, and all mankind, ... and in God the Holy Ghost, who *sanctifieth* me, and all the elect people of God.' For if these functions are made the basis of distinction between the Persons the conclusion is tritheism, and so classical Christian theology has insisted that they are no more than 'appropriations'. The Christian experience is of one God in three 'modes of being': yet these are not simply successive modes (Sabellianism). Nor are they merely true to our way of looking at it – so that 'ultimately' reality must be described otherwise (the doctrine of a purely 'economic' Trinity). And so one could go through all the various 'heresies', seen as false or inadequate transcripts of the existential relationship.

Positively, one can say that for the Christian the deepest awareness of ultimate reality, of what for him is most truly and finally real, can only be described *at one and the same time* in terms of the love of God *and* of the grace of our Lord Jesus Christ *and* of the fellowship of the Holy Spirit. All these are equally true and equally deep insights into and understandings of reality, and yet they all palpably express and define *one* reality, not competing realities. None is before or after, in the sense that one is a deeper truth than the others – so that one is 'divine', and the others merely human. In contrast, the unitarian would say that for him only one mode of experience is ultimate: Jesus is not a window through into ultimate reality (he is a man and no more), just as the fellowship of the Spirit is nothing more, nothing deeper, than human fellowship. But the Trinitarian Christian insists that he cannot from his experience deny that in *each* of these he meets the unconditional. Something that holds these three together is for him the only satisfactory model of final truth and reality. The deepest of all mysteries cannot be expressed in terms which deny ultimacy to any of these.

The doctrine of the Trinity is about God. But except on the 'supranaturalist projection' it is not the description of *a* Being – so that we have to visualize a sort of Divine triangle or Divine society 'existing' somewhere 'out there' or 'up there'. It is a description of Being, as it is known 'in Christ'. It is the final Christian definition of reality, the 'Christian name' (as Karl Barth puts it) of God. The doctrine is to the experienced reality what the map is to the earth or a model for the scientist. Inevitably, it will desiccate and distort. But it is better to have a map than no map, and to have a true map than a false. Hence the importance of Trinitarian doctrine. But it is equally important to be able to see the map for what it is. It is a transcript. Its truths are truths about the relational experience and are 'readings' from it: they are not statements about metaphysical entities beyond our ken.

Part of the article 'The Debate Continues', first published in *The Honest to God Debate*, SCM Press, 1963.

Concerning Theism

David Jenkins

I assume that the '*Honest to God* debate' is sufficiently shown to be an urgently necessary one by the response which the original book has evoked. The evidence of my own contacts and those of many of my friends is sufficient to convince me that the approach of the book has encouraged many people to feel able to look again, with a very real possibility of discovery, at questions concerning God, the meaning and context of life, and the practice and possibility of religion. Persons who have felt encouraged and set free by the example of the book to renew their quest into these matters include both some who have hitherto 'written off' all talk of God and all practice of religion and some who have succeeded in clinging with more or less difficulty and desperation to a 'faith' and the practices of a faith which they have not dared to investigate deeply because they have more than half suspected that under investigation the 'faith' will collapse. Thus the book constitutes an occasion of liberation and advance, whatever occasions of stumbling it may also be in danger of offering.

This being so, merely negative criticism would be a disaster and a faithless and disobedient throwing away of the opportunities opened up. But genuinely to further this discussion, full and careful use must be made of the resources at our disposal. At some stage in the continuing search for, and witness to, the truth about God and the world, a careful and extended contribution needs to be made which will show that one main strand in traditional Christian theism has always been concerned to deny or at least to be very cautious about precisely those features of 'theism' (e.g. being misled by the concept of God as *a* being or *a* person) which the Bishop rails against. There is an immense amount of material in the Fathers, both Western and Eastern, which, taken along with the insights of the great mystical writers and masters of the spiritual life, should remind us first very sharply and then very profitably of the scandalous poverty of much current 'theism'. The true extent of the scandal is peculiarly well shown by the fact that not only does the theism against which the Bishop protests seem to very many people to be recognizably the theism of the Christian church (and the only possible theism – hence the need and justification for atheism) but also the Bishop actually seems to be trapped in this belief himself. His attempt to be honest to God is so dishonest to the God of, for example, Athanasius or the fourth century Cappadocian writers or of Thomas Aquinas, let alone Augustine or, again, to the God of the author of the *Cloud of Unknowing* or, say, to the God who is worshipping in and through the shape of the Orthodox Liturgy, that it is clearly high time that we were confronted by an explosive reminder of the need to 'get our theism right'. It must not, however, be taken for granted that we can do this by forgetting all the traditional language because we superficially focus attention on its imagery and ignore its insights. Certainly the Bishop is in no position to be our guide here, as he is plainly ignorant of, or indifferent to, what has been said and what has been meant by what has been said. But this, in so far as it is true, must be taken not as a satisfactory criticism or refutation of what the Bishop has said, but as a challenge to those who are more familiar with those insights to bring them to bear on the situation which the Bishop indicates and exemplifies.

As I have neither time nor space here and now to take up my own challenge I wish, as a contribution to the continuing debate and as a prelude to the type of enterprise I have asked for, to try to show that it is extremely unlikely that the way forward will lead to a restatement of Christian belief which is in any way 'the end of theism' or the giving up of the notion of God as personal. It may be that I am committed to arguing in this way not by the points to which I shall later draw attention but entirely by my own personal predilections. For while I very greatly sympathize with and believe that I share in the Bishop's bewilderment, agnosticism and protests, I would not, I think, spontaneously or even on consideration, state the position from which I face and attack these bewilderments as he does. When he says (and again I find myself in agreement) that often in debates between Christians and humanists his 'sympathies are on the humanist's side' he goes on to say: 'This is not in the least because my faith or commitment is in doubt' (p. 8). The difficulty I find with this statement is that, for me, 'faith' implies 'faith in', and 'commitment' implies 'commitment to'. I do not think this is just a question of language – or, alternatively, if it is, it is a point to be followed up because, in one sense, the whole discussion is about language – about how we should talk and have grounds for talking about 'ultimate realities'. I feel a similar disquiet when he says (p. 27): 'I have never really doubted the fundamental truth of the Christian faith – though I have constantly found myself questioning its expression.' I am unable to be at all clear what it is that the Bishop has never really doubted. I do not think one could be altogether blamed for being inclined to deduce that what the Bishop has never doubted is that somehow or other his own 'attitude' or 'feeling' or 'commitment' is 'right'. If this suspicion were at all justified then one might not be very far from having to conclude that the one thing that the Bishop is, deep down, clear about is that he cannot be basically wrong – although it is not really clear what is the nature of this 'not-wrongness'.

Now this is almost certainly not only unfair but also verging on the unkind. None the less it may serve to bring out the point that whatever the difficulties about objective language in talk about God there are also very grave ones in subjective language. The only way I can describe my own attitude to, and in, the doubtings and difficulties to which the Bishop so rightly and with such evident sincerity directs our attention seems to be this. Even in moments of complete intellectual – and still worse, moral – bafflement, or when I feel wholehearted assent to a 'humanist' case apparently over against a 'Christian' one, I am still unable to doubt my faith *in God* and if I could in any way direct or control my commitment I would wish it to be commitment *to God*. Indeed I think I would go so far as to say that I do not really care about the truth, fundamentally or otherwise, of the 'Christian faith'. I am only concerned with whatever the Christian faith is in so far as it helps on the question of God, his being, his nature and the possibility of relationship to him. I am, it is true, thus far only describing my attitude, and it may quite plausibly be argued that this attitude is (*a*) subjectively immature and (*b*) objectively wrong. But the fact that it is possible to attack it on, say, Freudian or existentialist grounds under (*a*) is not the same thing as proving (*b*) – unless one holds that the only possible theory of knowledge (as a whole, not merely knowledge of God) is the extreme existentialist position or that Freudian insights define and exhaust reality. I may perhaps, therefore, be allowed to maintain for the purposes of the argument that my attitude has built into it an objective reference to God, although I should add that 'God' operates not so much as the name of an object but much more like a proper name. (I understand faith in or commitment to persons or causes. I do not understand, or perhaps rather do not accept, the notion of faith in or commitment to an object. That certainly is idolatry – or insanity.)

If I try to maintain such a position, including that my attitude is a 'proper' attitude (i.e. is related to truth, to the way things really are), I clearly lay myself open to plain and straightforward contradiction powerfully urged. 'You say that you are unable to doubt your commitment to a *personal God*. That may be your psychological state but it is a regrettable one (or at least a delusion if that is not necessarily regrettable). There is no God.' I have in fact demonstrated just what Tillich says (quoted by Robinson, p. 57): 'The first step to atheism is always a theology which drags God down to the level of doubtful things.' This may be so, but I very much fear that there is a real sense in which the existence of God *is* doubtful (i.e. capable of being doubted), that atheism will always seem a real existential possibility, and that this remains so even if you attempt to restate the doctrine of God in terms of 'ultimate concern' and the like. In this connection a remark of the Bishop's is very instructive (p. 29): 'God is, by definition, ultimate reality. And one cannot argue whether ultimate reality *exists*.' We have, I think, detected some very determinedly anti-traditional-metaphysic thinkers trying to get away with a concealed and possibly inverted version of the traditional ontological argument. (This is the argument that the *Idea* of God includes the idea of existing and so God *must* exist. The mistake in this has usually been supposed to be that while the *idea* of God may include the *idea* of existing the fact that people have *ideas* of a certain sort is, of itself, no evidence at all that anything corresponding to the ideas *really* exists.) Of course you cannot argue whether ultimate reality exists. You can only ask whether pretentious phrases like 'ultimate reality' are wanted at all and, *a fortiori*, whether there is any case for bringing the word 'God' within smelling distance of the argument. Moreover the 'ultimate reality' or 'ultimate concern' of Robinson and of Tillich (in the quotations Robinson uses) is no more an obvious, self-evident or demonstrably necessary feature of the world or of our experiences in the world than God is.

Thus Robinson continues the passage I have just referred to (p. 29): '... one cannot argue whether ultimate reality *exists*. One can only ask what ultimate reality is like ...' It is quite clear that the answer he wishes to maintain as the true answer to *that* question is by no means self-evident, and if it is not self-evident it is, of course, doubtful and deniable (like the God of the theism he is wondering whether to repudiate). For example, on p. 49 he writes: 'To believe in God as love means to believe that in pure personal relationship we encounter, not merely what ought to be, but what is, the deepest, veriest truth about the structure of reality. This, in face of all the evidence, is a tremendous act of faith. But it is not the feat of persuading oneself of the existence of a super-Being beyond this world endowed with personal qualities. Belief in God is the trust, the well-nigh incredible trust, that to give ourselves to the uttermost in love is not to be confounded but to be "accepted", that Love is the ground of our being, to which ultimately we "come home".' 'In face of all the evidence', 'the well-nigh incredible trust' and so on make it quite clear that talk about the existence of ultimate reality not being arguable is irrelevant bluff. 'Ultimate reality' is a trivial and meaningless phrase until you begin to characterize 'it', and the character the Bishop (and Tillich) want to give 'it' is something over and above 'it' where 'it' is just plain matter of fact reality (the 'stuff' that is 'all the evidence'). They say, in fact, that 'it' is to be described in 'personal categories', and that 'Love is the ground of our being'. Since *all* human conduct is manifestly not loving, and it is very doubtful in what sense any of the processes of the physical universe could ordinarily be so described, it begins to appear that 'ultimate reality' is logically very much like a phrase describing an 'object' which is 'other than' the objects we actually encounter, even if it is thought of as 'underlying' rather than 'being above' the phenomenal world.

The fact that this 'ground' is 'something' which is other than the stuff of our ordinary life and existence even if it is in that ordinary stuff that 'it' is encountered is made clear enough at numerous points, despite repeated statements which try to equate the two. Compare for example the quotation above where 'Love' suddenly gets a capital letter and we are said to be 'accepted' and 'come home', even if only in inverted commas (i.e. it is at least *as if* we were in a personal relationship with the Other – why not then a (carefully guarded) conception of a personal God?). Further, we are warned that 'the eternal *Thou* is not to be equated with the finite *Thou*, nor God with man or nature' (p. 53), just after we have been told (correctly on the basis of the First Epistle of John) that the statement that 'God is love' is not reversible, i.e. God is the subject and love is the predicate. But all this is surely to say that as a matter of logic we are justified in maintaining what, as Christians, we do about the Universe and life in the Universe because God exists and because he is love. What Tillich and Robinson following him are talking about is *how* we (or some of us modern 'we's') come or may come to maintain what we do, but this is different from *what* we maintain.

But the logical difficulties of theism are not even clarified, let alone removed by their procedure. Indeed, a good deal of the language seems in danger of being less clear and, thereby, possibly more dishonest than some more traditional statements. Take, for example, the extended quotation from Tillich on p. 81, where the talk is of grace. Grace is carefully referred to as 'it' but 'it' behaves in a very personal way (and, indeed, since the 'happenings' involved are said not to be at our command it looks very much as if grace 'comes in from outside' – at any rate from outside us). The situation referred to is 'as though a voice were saying "You are accepted"'. Now 'seeming to be addressed' and still more 'accepting the fact that we are accepted' sounds like descriptions of a personal relationship with a being who is at least personal, and we may perhaps believe that this *is* what is being pointed to, as later on the term 'Ground' gets a capital 'G', which suggests that perhaps it is being treated as very like a proper name. Again, statements like 'we all know that we are bound eternally and inescapably to the Ground of our being' (cited on p. 80) are just not true save where 'we all' means 'all we who believe in an eternal personal God who will not let us go'. If, for example, 'we all' meant 'I and my friends' then there would be some who would hold that any 'I' is simply a temporary and temporal collocation of matter who could only be spoken of as 'bound eternally and inescapably to the Ground of our being', in so far as it is true that matter or energy cannot be created or destroyed. (A very doubtful proposition, I believe.)

I should maintain, therefore, that the traditional theistic talk about a personal God is no more (although admittedly no less) *logically* difficult than is the talk about 'ultimate reality' and 'ultimate concern' which is urged upon us. For *as used* the term 'ultimate reality' no more refers to some self-evident existence than does the name 'God'. One can refuse or be unable to believe in God and one can refuse or be unable to believe that 'ultimate reality' has the character asserted.

Further, *if* ultimate reality does have the character asserted of 'it', then it looks very much as if it remains true that there exists a personal God who is other than and more than the stuff and phenomena of our life, however true it must be that he is to be encountered only in and through this stuff.

Hence the task to which the Bishop of Woolwich's book and the response to it summon us is that of re-deepening our theism by drawing much more fully on the rich and deep truths of the Christian tradition, always with a full consciousness of the difficulties and demands which modern insights make upon us (although by no means all these demands are in essence new; I suspect that the only thing which has always counted decisively against the difficulty of believing in God is that as a matter of fact he exists and makes himself known).

In connection with this task I would like to add two brief postscripts. First, it is by no means self-evident that images of depth are richer or more satisfactory than images of height – and that especially in the area of personal relationships and personal development. Here is a matter for urgent discussion between psychologists and theologians. How far does 'depth' imagery correlate with desires to escape from reality as it is manifested in persons, to 'return to the womb' and to get away from the stretching demands of integration in relation with, and with reference to, others? And how far does 'height' stand for the demand always to go further than every outgoing experience wherein the self is expressed on behalf of other selves? Ought we to understand that over and above going 'deeper into ourselves' our *real* end [ultimate concern?] is to reach out and, so to speak, up far beyond ourselves to a fulfilment which embraces all persons? It might perhaps be true that the problem of transcendence is the problem of the fulfilment of human personality in a fullness of personality that embraces all personal possibilities in a Transcendent which (who) is fully personal. To this end the best symbolism might be the challenge of height symbolism. Perhaps it may turn out that the doctrine of the Trinity (the transcendent 'personalness' of God which is more than 'persons' and yet the perfection of unified personality) is not all that irrelevant psychologically, metaphysically or theologically.

And secondly, if the conviction that ultimate reality is love does require us to continue to believe in a personal God (or does depend for its truth on the existence of a personal God – whichever way we happen to or always have to come to the truth), then it may very well turn out that the material which the Bishop brings to bear in his fourth chapter on the question of christology is again to be used to re-enliven rather than replace the traditional understanding of the person of Jesus.

For example, on p. 74 Robinson writes: 'It is in Jesus, and Jesus alone, that there is nothing of self to be seen, but solely the ultimate, unconditional love of God. It is as he emptied himself utterly of himself that he became the carrier of "the name which is above every name", the revealer of the Father's glory – for that name and that glory is simply Love.' But Love is the ultimate reality of the Universe who is God. If one were wanting to relate this directly to the traditional way of stating Christian doctrine (based on the Greek language of the third and fourth Christian centuries) one could point out that 'ultimate reality' could legitimately be tied up with the Greek word *hypostasis* ('that which stands under', 'what in each individual case is really there'). One would want to make this tie up because *hypostasis* is the traditional word for the 'persons' of the Trinity and for the 'person' of Jesus Christ. But since this ultimate reality is rightly thought of as personal (i.e. *is* – really – Love) and since Jesus is 'solely the ultimate, unconditional love of God', is it not legitimate to say that the *hypostasis* who is Jesus (i.e. the *reality* of the person who is called 'Jesus') is, as the creed says, 'of one substance with the Father' (i.e. a real expression of the reality which/who is God)? For Jesus is the perfect, particular, personal expression of the underlying personal reality of the Universe. Further, as the Bishop indicates in his talk of 'emptied himself utterly of himself', we are now in a position to have a much richer understanding of the traditional doctrine of the divine self-emptying in Jesus. For if love is 'existence for others' then to be 'really Love' (an 'hypostasis' who is 'of one substance' with the Father) is identical with existing wholly for others and emptying oneself of one's own self-existence to that end, so that the human personal existence of Jesus *is* the divine existence in the terms of our limited and creaturely existence.

This is not just theological word-play or logic-chopping, but is closely related to this matter of a 'tremendous act of faith' or 'the well-nigh incredible trust' of which the Bishop (on p. 49) speaks with some enthusiasm but which rather troubles me. Certainly I believe that the decision on what ultimate reality is really like demands what is always an act of faith, i.e. you decide to 'back' and indeed to 'put your trust in' some part of the evidence that is lying about as the crucial clue to the whole (which human concern is really ultimate, which facet of reality – things as they hit me and others – is directly and decisively related to ultimate reality, etc.). This is a similar decision whether you decide that it is physical explanation which is ultimate or Love or what you will. But acts of faith and trust are not to be commended for being 'tremendous' or 'well-nigh incredible'. To be anything other than irresponsible escapism they must have grounds. And one very powerful ground for deciding that ultimate reality is Love is belief in God and one of the most powerful grounds for believing in God is Jesus, especially Jesus as both the climax of a long tradition of belief in God and the source of such a tradition. Hence 'who Jesus really is' is directly linked with 'what is the nature of ultimate reality'.

Of course there are very great difficulties in all this. In particular I am personally convinced that the Bishop's strictures about traditional christology in practice being alarmingly and misleadingly monophysite (i.e. treating Jesus as God absorbing and in effect removing human nature) are far more generally true than his strictures on the practice of theism (which are true enough). But I wished simply to give a brief indication in the area of christology of my general thesis which is that the way forward to do justice to the insights and challenges perceived and conveyed by such as Tillich, Bonhoeffer and, in their steps, the Bishop of Woolwich, lies in taking very seriously, far more seriously than is current practice over an alarmingly large area of the church, the insights and assertions of the continuing Christian tradition. For our primary concern is surely not that 'they', whoever they are, should agree with 'us', whoever 'we' are, but that 'we' and 'they' should together be taken beyond our present partial insights and errors nearer to the wholeness of understanding which is truth.

To this end total surrender to what are alleged to be the 'necessary' ways for modern thinking is likely to be as stultifying and misleading as is abject and unreflective clinging to older statements and ways of thinking treated as mere formulae. But in so far as they represent an understanding of God and ultimate reality which our fathers wrested from their own encounters with life and with God we surely neglect them at our peril. I believe that the Bishop is wholly right to seek to shock the church into really awakening to the fact that the way we look at the world we live in must be radically different from the views acceptable to those who lived before us. But if there is any sense in talking about God at all we can scarcely suppose that we shall know what we may *truthfully* say if we neglect what others have, under the pressure of their ultimate concerns, learnt to say of the God who was ultimate reality to them.

First published in *The Honest to God Debate*, SCM Press 1963.

By-passing the Transformer Stations

F. Gerald Downing

Normally in this country, theological currents pass through many transformer stations before they reach 'lay' homes; and in many places, such stations have never been built, or if built, they have fallen into disrepair. And there are many Luddites who applaud this state of affairs, for currents are very dangerous things, and people should be insulated from them, if not by design, then at least by accident. If you try to by-pass the transformer stations you may get a very exciting short-circuit: there is a bright flash, and then all goes dead. On the other hand, you may find many of the lay homes and the local churches have all along been wired to stand very high tension indeed, and your dangerous act may by-pass the natural and artificial resistances, and produce a glad and warm light.

Apologies for the cumbrous allegory – especially if the physics are incorrect.

There are now two ways of evaluating this book. Because it has broken through the normal channels, just to look at it for its academic value, its consistency and so on, and just to gauge its likely usefulness, is not enough. What effect has it had, even at the time of writing? It received welcoming reviews from Jack Lucas in the *Daily Herald*, and from Christopher Driver in *The Guardian*. It was received with cold disapproval by the *Daily Mail*, which asked the obvious question, 'Ought this man to be a Bishop?', and this was the only outside comment quoted by the *Church Times*, for whom it was 'the national press'. Here Bishop Wand's comments were rather saner, if shallow; but the editor obviously disapproved of this 'charitable review'.

Comment in *The Observer* elicited from leading churchmen was varied, and (this confessedly) not always fully informed; but this was only representative of the wider public reaction. There was a huge response based only on garbled reports in papers, and hurried interviews on television. The inaccuracy of the impression may be judged from some letters in the *Daily Herald*, 22 March. 'I share the ideas of the Bishop of Woolwich ... That is why I am not a member of the Church of England.' 'The Bishop would be completely at home in the Unitarian Church.' 'Spiritualists ... have been giving teaching similar to that of the Bishop for many years.' 'Most Salvation Army officers and soldiers would say "Amen" to the Bishop's views, as quoted, on the redemptive death of Jesus.'

These representatives of varied religious traditions may be right, and I may have long been misunderstanding them. But I think that the initial publicity has given a confused picture. Only if it results in the book being read and thought about will it in this way become a 'good book'. But if this is the result, it may be a very good book indeed.

The book has shorted the usual circuits; but the fuses down at consumer level look as if they will hold. In the book, then, John Robinson writes for those who seek to *live* as Christians, but for whom tradition has provided no usable words to express or to focus their Christianity. He writes for those for whom atheism is the only genuine possibility in the face of the unmeaning and even plain moral inadequacy of much Christian talk of God; whether their atheism be relieved or reluctant. He writes for ordinary Christians who would come to terms with a secular culture, which is the culture of the real world, the world as it is.

He would abolish the supernaturalism that relegates the divine to an easily avoidable, because quite irrelevant, realm that is half-physically, half-symbolically 'out there'. He would discard a theology that (by its devotion to imagery drawn from an outworn picture of the Universe) bids fair to make for us an idol rather than point us to God. He would have us break out of a cramping religiosity that attempts to domesticate the transcendent, confine it to a tiny private sector of a few men's lives, and guard it jealously for them alone.

He attempts to be honest; especially to be honest to the person who asks, 'What do you *really* believe? Is your faith strong enough to stand today; or is it a mummy that would crumble to dust if you stripped off the tattered bandages that seem to surround it – the protective layer of people afraid, clergy entrenched, and the good-natured tolerance of *de mortuis nil nisi bonum*?'

The sheer life and light that come from reading the theologians quoted here (and the others to which they in turn introduce you) have been too long confined to universities and theological colleges. 'It would not do for the fifth form. Still less would it go in the parish.' Even if you disagree with the book, even if everyone found it was largely wrong; if it does let these ideas break out of the few specialized circuits they run round in this country, it will be very good.

But when all this is said, to be honest I must confess that as a 'recasting' of the faith, I think the book fails. It fails because it tries to pit only the strongest sectors of Paul Tillich's new religion against only the weakest sectors of traditional Christianity. The hymnals, for instance, contain the immanence of *Saint Patrick's Breastplate* as well as the absentee transcendence of *Come down, O Love Divine*. Again, it is possible to distrust the community's *account* of its prayer, without refusing to trust its practice; and the practice starts to suggest a better and quite realistic rationale, if you maintain it.

But it is the brave effort to combine so many modern theologians that brings the most serious failure. On p. 86, note 2, Dr Robinson tries to clear up the difficulty that arises when Paul Tillich seems very much in favour of 'religion', and Dietrich Bonhoeffer would discard it. We are told that Bonhoeffer's is a 'narrower sense', and that this sort of religion Tillich would not countenance either.

But this is not true, even for passages quoted from the two in the text of the book. Bonhoeffer is allowed to say on p. 36: 'Christian apologetic has taken the most varying forms of opposition to this (modern) self-assurance. Efforts are made to prove to a world thus come of age that it cannot live without the tutelage of "God". Even though there has been surrender on all secular problems, there still remain the so-called ultimate questions – death, guilt – on which only "God" can furnish an answer... Thus we (clergy and theologians) live to some extent by these ultimate questions of humanity. But what if one day they no longer exist as such, if they too can be answered without "God"?' And there could hardly be a greater contrast with the passages from Tillich quoted later (pp. 79–82): 'We always remain in the power of that from which we are estranged. The fact brings us to the ultimate depth of sin: separated and yet bound, estranged and yet belonging, destroyed and yet preserved, the state which is called despair... Grace strikes us when we are in great pain and restlessness. It strikes us when we walk through the dark valley of a meaningless and empty life ...' Dr Robinson noted that Bonhoeffer did not find Rudolf Bultmann's 'de-mythologizing' adequate in the modern situation (p. 36). He could have noted that Bonhoeffer also found it necessary to reject the efforts of Tillich, and I think the latter's post-war theology is similar enough to make the remark relevant: 'Tillich set out to interpret the evolution of the world itself – against its will – in a religious sense, to give it its whole shape through religion. That was very courageous of him, but the world unseated him and went on by itself: he too sought to understand the world better than it understood itself, but it felt entirely misunderstood, and rejected the imputation.' You have to decide – whichever way your decision goes – between Tillich who would have everything religious, and would wait for a man to grow weak so that he might talk to him; and Bonhoeffer who expected 'an entire absence of religion', and if he spoke Christian ideas at all, would want to speak to a man in his strength, at the centre of life – not on the edge of despair, where I guess he would just have cared for him. When Tillich says the word 'God' is too meaningless to keep using, he goes off and talks at length in other terms; Bonheoffer prefers silence.

In effect, Dr Robinson prefers Tillich. Is he right to? He wants to talk to modern man; he wants to talk truth. Now obviously, Tillich does get through to some, and deserves to, for his sympathies are with the whole of modern man's life. But I venture the guess that Bonhoeffer was right, and that in the main modern man is interested in, if you will, 'penultimate' things, not 'ultimate'; he does not even find language about 'the ground of being' that is 'beyond being' sufficiently clear to be able either to agree or disagree with Tillich. He does not know what Tillich is saying. Julian Huxley in *The Observer*, 31 March, was right to call this language 'semantic cheating, and so vague as to be effectively meaningless'. Although Dr Robinson is right to suggest that much linguistic analysis of talk about 'God' has been concerned with peripheral examples, Tillich's translation into abstract categories is no help at all. It is just as vulnerable, some think more so. The linguistic philosopher represents 'the modern man' and, by and large, he can make no sense of Tillich. This means, too, that Tillichian theology is no real defence against a naturalistic humanism (as contributors to the symposium quoted above make clear). The *impression* that Tillich gives is of an atheistic idealist naturalism based on the last century, with frequent purely formal, verbally confusing protests that this is not what he intends. This is the *impression* he gives. He may be on to real, Christian truth of 'God' and 'the universe', but he just has not yet found convincing ways of showing most Christians or most non-Christians that this is so. For the time being, his ontology, his abstract defence of 'transcendence', is too unsure a horse to back, especially in a popular book.

Of course, Tillich has much else to say that is good, true, and useful; and of course we would gratefully pay the same tribute to Dr Robinson's book. But (irrespective of the still debated question of the 'truth' of Tillich's position), it is unlikely for the present that the ontological mysticism that Dr Robinson accepts from Tillich as the 'theological' substance of the book will appeal to more than the few who are only at home with abstract thought. It is not 'childish' to think pictorially; it is a constant feature of the mental life of a certain proportion of people, intelligent or dim, adult or child. A large proportion can think either way (graphically or abstractly). But then (at least for most) to talk of an abstract 'loving', to talk of 'love' exercised by one who is not 'a being' does not say anything at all. The word 'love' is completely evacuated of meaning. Every attempt to make 'God' 'more than personal' succeeds only in making him (it?) less; impersonal, an object, and so, unable 'to love' or 'to be love'. In one quite frequent sense of 'myth' (any non-empirical frame of reference by which we attempt to interpret all that is), Tillich's ontology is only another form of myth (compare Hinduism, which also has both pictorial and abstract myths). It suffers from all the linguistic disabilities of myth, with a few extra confusions added. It is likely to leave a great many people cold.

Tillich gives the impression of wanting 'religion' without 'God'; Bonhoeffer wants 'Christianity' without 'religion'. It is attempts to make sense of the latter (rather than Tillich, or for that matter, Huxley) that may become meaningful to modern man. For the moment, most Christians do want to retain some sort of myth, pictorial or abstract. The one thing that they are likely to find difficult is holding to either sort while believing it untrue. The reviewer must admit that he does believe the traditional pictorial and dramatic 'myths' of Christendom 'true', while hoping to be able to interpret them as Dietrich Bonhoeffer proposed, in a totally 'secular' way.

And this may be the way the Bishop would really have us go; for he makes it clear that the test for worship – and so, we may deduce, for any other activity of Christians among themselves, including thinking and theologizing – is 'how far it makes us *more sensitive* ... to the Christ in the hungry, the naked, the homeless and the prisoner' (p. 90). This *is* a secular interpretation, if the words we have omitted are left unsaid.

As a theological statement (even as a theological reconnoitre), the book probably fails. It is not so much that (as the Bishop thought might be) it is 'not radical enough', though that too may be true; it is that it is not radical in the right direction. Yet as a stimulant, as a programme for action, widely accepted, it would be tremendous.

First published in *Prism*, May 1963 and reprinted in *The Honest to God Debate*.

The One Thing Needful

Alec Graham

Honest to God is an attempt to help us discover the one thing needful. We may disregard some of the Bishop's Aunt Sallies; it is hard to believe, for instance, that many Christians really do think of divine transcendence in spatial terms: we recognize that hymns which speak of Jesus 'far above yon azure height' or as 'a Friend for little children above the bright blue sky' express in terms of spatial distance what we should prefer to put in terms of spiritual otherness. Furthermore, few, if any, communicants really do think of God as 'out there' beyond the east end of the church rather than as powerfully active in the eucharistic action. But it would be foolish for us to let ourselves be irritated by these Aunt Sallies, for if we sit at the Bishop's feet, we may hear him reminding us of disturbing truths which it is comfortable for us to forget. We sometimes hear complaints that there is no open vision in our day, but perhaps at last we are witnessing a rebirth of prophecy, and we should be careful not to quench it before its disquieting message can make us once again aware of the one thing needful.

The Bishop reminds us that we should not think of God as a Person or a Being. We might go one step further and remind ourselves that when we talk about 'Three Persons in One God', we certainly do not use the word Person in the way in which we use it in everyday speech. Again, the Bishop reminds us that the Chalcedonian Definition does not exhaust or explain the mystery of the person of the incarnate Lord. It is unlikely that the fathers of Chalcedon themselves ever thought that it did, but it is just as well for us to be reminded that we cannot explain the mystery of his person in fifth-century terminology, or, for that matter, in twentieth-century terminology. There was at least a generally accepted philosophical terminology in the fifth century, which is more than can be said for the twentieth century, but no human terminology can ever adequately do justice to the mystery of the Lord's person or to the mystery of the threefold being of God. Those who have met and known the living God on their knees and in their lives have always recognized this. In Isaiah we read 'My thoughts are not your thoughts, neither are your ways my ways, saith the Lord. For as the heavens are higher than the earth, so are my ways higher than your ways, and my thoughts than your thoughts.' Augustine tells us that 'the supereminence of the Godhead surpasses the power of customary speech': therefore we say something only lest we say nothing. Some of the Eastern fathers were even apprehensive about saying that God is one, for he is ineffable; but if we are to talk about him at all, then we have to use language which must by its very nature be inadequate; and the language which we normally use is the language of analogy. We have Jesus' own authority for doing this: 'when you pray, say, Our Father . . .' or 'the kingdom of heaven is like . . .' The Bishop of Woolwich uses his analogies of love and depth; but every use of analogy has its difficulties, for if we are asked to be precise and say what is the exact point of resemblance in any particular analogy, we find that we are often in difficulties and that we can do no more than reply that God may be said to be like us in such and such respects, but that his ways and thoughts are so far removed from ours that we cannot be any more precise. Of course we possess and have to use the commonly accepted trinitarian and christological formulae, but the Bishop has caused us to look at them again and to think about them. He has made us ask ourselves whether orthodoxy in the generally accepted sense of the term is the one thing needful which it is so often supposed to be, or whether it may well in fact be for some of us a convenient line of least resistance which saves us from coming face to face with all sorts of difficulties concerning the nature and grounds of faith.

Again, the Bishop reminds us (and we can never be reminded of this too frequently) that prayer and worship are not activities separate from real life and that living and praying are not two activities which should be carefully prevented from meeting. It is true that some people nowadays treat the church and its worship as an escape from the hard demands of life, and no doubt some people have done this in every age; so it is important for us to be reminded that the one thing needful is not the mere observance of religious duties. The classic example of the man who thought that the outward performance of his religious duties was the one thing needful is the Pharisee in the parable of the Pharisee and the Publican, but if we find ourselves saying, 'Of course, I'm not like the Pharisee', then the time has come for us to realize that we are. Most of us probably need to hear again and again the Bishop's message that we must not compartmentalize the sacred and the secular, religion and life, worship and work. Probably many of us need to take seriously to heart the prophetic message which is now being ever more loudly proclaimed that worship so far from being the one thing needful can be an activity which presents us from meeting and responding to the active, living God, who all the time stands over against us and seeks to elicit from us the response of self-giving trust.

But it is not only the one thing needful in belief and worship which the Bishop tries to lay bare for us: he also recalls us to the message of the Summary of the Law as the basis of all Christian conduct. Just as he would not let us take refuge in credal definitions or in formal worship, so here he will not let us be content with rules for Christian conduct: a Christian's behaviour cannot be adequately prescribed by rules any more than God can be adequately described in words. All along the line, in matters of belief and worship and conduct, the Bishop reminds us that the rules of thumb are no more than rules of thumb, and we must be careful not to place our reliance on these rules instead of on him who stands behind them and above them.

One feels that the Bishop might well have gone further and reminded us how many other familiar landmarks give the Christian only a rough indication of what he should be believing or doing. He might well have drawn our attention to the difficulties of being certain about exactly what Jesus said and did: for instance, the very words translated 'one thing needful' in most of our English versions present textual problems about which it is impossible to be dogmatic. Or, if we ask why did God create the world, why did he choose to use such an apparently wasteful method as the evolutionary process, why do men suffer, what do we mean by the fall or original sin, then we have to realize that in the long run we cannot be content with any of the answers which are conventionally given, for at long last Christians are learning a little humility and they are not quite so ready with all sorts of speculative answers. It is only when we see or experience suffering that we can find any answer to some of these questions, but we do not find it in terms of a neat formula which we can hand on to other people and which they can correctly pass on to others. For some people it is only beside the cross that any answer at all is possible to the insoluble problems of life, and even then the answer will not be capable of proper expression in conceptual terms.

Perhaps we are reminded of Bishop Lightfoot's statement, 'I find that my faith suffers nothing by leaving a thousand questions open, so long as I am convinced on two or three main lines.' One of these main lines must be that in the New Testament we read of One who calls us to be his followers and seeks from us the response of self-giving trust, that this trust admits us to a close relationship with him (which, like all relationships between people, cannot be adequately described in words and in which there must be many questions left open) and that this trust needs to be constantly renewed and kept supple by repeated acts of self-giving in prayer, sacrament and action. Of this self-giving the action of the lad in St John's account of the feeding of the 5,000 is perhaps typical: his gifts seemed insignificant by comparison with the crowd's need, but he surrendered them to Jesus, who used them in a totally unexpected way. Is not this the one thing needful? Not merely to sit at Jesus' feet and hear his word, but to surrender oneself wholly to him, to be completely devoted to him as no doubt was Mary, the sister of Martha. But the act of devotion at Jesus' feet is not all there is in this act of self-surrender, for in it is included the surrender of our time and money and ability to meeting human need, to obeying the imperative of the parable of the Good Samaritan.

And if we prefer, as the Bishop of Woolwich does, to act first and to withdraw in prayer afterwards, who can say we are wrong? Our devotion in prayer and our devotion in action are equally components of our worship and self-surrender: properly speaking, they should be indistinguishable from one another: *laborare est orare*, and *vice versa*. Perhaps the one thing needful is as simple as that, and the Bishop of Woolwich has done us all the service of reminding us of it.

First published in the *Cowley Evangelist*, May 1963 and reprinted in *The Honest to God Debate*.

Women's Voices

The Honest to God Debate contained a chapter which quoted, by permission, the letters which readers of *Honest to God* wrote to John Robinson. Here are some, all of these from women.

Some correspondents wrote from outside the church:

> I wonder where you feel people like me belong? Perhaps if I were inside the church I could stay there, but I cannot make the step into the church as I find it here. I find myself more immediately at home with humanists and yet I know that I have a conviction about love, which is faith and won't do in a purely humanistic setting.
>
> Perhaps for myself I could accept the position of outsider, but I have four young children and I wish somehow we could shelter under the Christian umbrella.

From an old lady:

> I as a child and young girl took religion very seriously. At sixteen I began to question, and as time went on so the questions went on and on, and were gently pushed to the back of my mind for many years. Later I openly acknowledged my break with the church's teaching, for instance the Virgin Birth. I would ask myself if I believed in God. I did not know, so I called myself a Humanist. I am now a pensioner, and I believe in truth and beauty with a faith that makes life worth while, for in spite of the misery and pain there is also much goodness. Perhaps this faith is not too far apart from progressive teaching within the church?

A woman wrote from Canterbury:

> I personally found the chapters on prayers and church-going in particular removed a vast load of guilt and misery. So many of one's repeated efforts merely ended in failure and a despairing effort to do better next time, and then more failure and guilt.
>
> Unlike the mediaevals we are now educated to think for ourselves, and cannot help thinking about, questioning, and reading about all aspects of our belief, and finding things which strike with an inner certainty of truth. It is just so marvellous to have all this coming from a bishop of the church, and having one's thoughts and hopes confirmed, not rejected, from inside the church. I am certain this must help a great many thinking people to remain in the church, and to bring back others who have felt increasingly alienated from it.

A voice from the pews:

> I am simply an ordinary housewife with an ordinary history, but probably representative of many others, who like me have been inspired and encouraged by your book and who, like me, have not really got the time to write and tell you so.
>
> I started as a Roman Catholic but left the church and nearly all belief, as I thought then, forever at the age of twenty (1934). I came back into the Church of England five years ago when my children decided they wanted to be Christians and wanted me to be their witness. I had come back to a belief in God and prayer and the resurrection. I have continued to 'support' the church to the best of my ability although passionately dissatisfied and conscious that its symbolism at present is useless to my husband, friends, relatives, although they are all people who love truth and love and do not label themselves as anything, but are cut off from Christianity in England today.
>
> What is perhaps worse is that the younger generation, the ones who care most to reach the truth, cannot recognize it in the present 'mould'. I would not say that the church has 'nothing to lose but its chains' but it is peculiarly near to that, and I hope you have started a revolution.

A woman's voice from a vicarage:

> There are many causes for this indebtedness to your book, the greatest being your reconciliation of the divine and the human in Christ. The orthodox teaching has always maddened me; so many other humans have sacrificed themselves for us, endured more sustained and prolonged torture, without the comfort of being the 'favourite son'. If, however, as I have understood from your book, Christ's divinity lies in his struggle, as a mortal, and his success in emptying himself of self, so that God might shine through, this truly is of God. Any of us knows the impossibility of the struggle; what you have helped to remove is my constant annoyance that Christ always had an unfair advantage.
>
> Perhaps one of the greatest blessings is that you – and the men who have inspired you – have made the church seem alive again, when for years it has seemed so unbearably dead! My children, with the gap of one generation, are directly descended from parsons back to 1513. This is a heritage which has been of great support to me and I should like to pass it on as a living thing. I am much more hopeful now of being able to do so.

Another 'ordinary vicar's wife' wrote:

> Before reading it, I was full of fear and trepidation, expecting the foundations of my world to crumble. Just the reverse happened. I have never been so inspired and stimulated by a theological book in all my life. Although I don't pretend either to understand and agree with everything in it, the stimulation to think and clarify our thoughts was too uplifting, that for this reason alone it was worth reading.
>
> Like many others I have become a lazy thinker, and a book of this kind is a helpful and very necessary jolt – especially to people like myself who are intimately involved in the working of the church. All the rather irksome chores of being a vicar's wife (plus of course, the joyful ones) and the disappointments, etc., suddenly seem so much more worthwhile.
>
> I used to wonder so often if it was worth the effort, when Christianity seemed so far away from 'religion' (as you define

it). From the help given in your book, I can see a 'break-through'. I just hope that we on the church side of the fence have the courage and initiative to make it.

A less faithful churchgoer wrote:

As a husband, three daughters, an elderly aunt, three cats and a large old house take up rather a lot of my time, I have had to do most of my reading on top of a double decker bus on my way into town to do the shopping. Not the best place for trying to study a book of such depth, especially as not being a classical scholar I found some parts rather difficult and quite a number of words which needed looking up in the dictionary!

I can't tell you how much better I feel for having read it.

Ever since I can remember I have had doubts – I have never been able to go to a church service without having a wild desire in the middle of the sermon and sometimes the lessons to stand up and start asking questions which I felt sure to the average churchgoer, priest or layman, would sound utterly blasphemous. Yet to me these questions seemed to be begging for an answer, and as the years passed I just became more and more frustrated in my efforts to find God in church. It seemed to be the one and only place where I just couldn't get near to him at all. There seemed to be so many things which I was expected to believe and accept unquestioningly if I was to be a true member of the church and I found so many of them utterly illogical and to my way of thinking, unnecessary. The church seemed to make Christianity so terribly complicated when to me it seemed so simple.

About eight years ago I just gave up the struggle – I told my vicar that after much heart searching I had reached the conclusion that the only part of the service I could repeat and honestly believe was the first four words of the Apostles' Creed and in the circumstances I felt any further attempts to take part in church services would be extremely hypocritical. He was duly sympathetic and hoped I should continue to attend church as an example to my children (an example of what?!).

For some days after this decision I suffered pangs of guilt and secretly wondered if perhaps I was wrong after all and if the vengeful god of the Old Testament might perhaps strike me down any minute with some terrible affliction for my sins, but as the days passed I became aware of something stealing quietly into my life which I can only describe as 'that peace which the world cannot give'. It has remained with me constantly ever since.

Like you, I firmly believe that nothing can separate us from the love of God. It is with us, and around us and in the very depth of our being, and closing our eyes or ears to it can never send it away.

I suppose I am really a heretic in the eyes of the church, I don't really know. I certainly don't do all the things which my vicar considers essential for my salvation. I go to church periodically because my husband is in the choir, and I encourage my daughters to think and never stop searching for the Truth, and to see the love of God in all life.

I think what I have really been trying to say is that I believe there must be many ordinary people like myself who have just the same doubts and who long for the church to give them a helping hand, but who have become bogged down by the mixture of man-made dogma and ancient mythology which seems to be the present basis of Christianity. If only you would write another *Honest to God* in really simple layman's language that the simplest mind could read and digest, I think even you would be amazed at the number of kindred spirits you would find in the world.

No less candid was this letter:

I want to thank you for your book. To do so in a way that means anything much, I must tell you why. I should have written before if it were not for a deep-rooted habit of reticence about the things that matter to me most; and because I thought you might be deluged with such letters. But after reading what passed at Convocation, I think that you may well have received a good many letters and comments of another sort, and that my reticence should this time be overcome.

I've been married for over twenty-five years to an engineer. He has just retired from the Overseas Civil Service after thirty years in Africa. We have two children now at university and their education has meant that for ten years we were separated quite a lot. One of these long periods of separation coincided with the Hungarian Revolution. I was in England: I speak German and French, and I had a car. So I went to Austria to see what I could do; the children were at boarding-school. First I floundered about in the mud on the border and in a big reception camp, and after the Christmas holidays in England I went back to take charge of a camp for refugee students, men and girls from sixteen to twenty-five – about fifty of them. Ninety per cent had been fighting, all were in a highly nervous state. They quarrelled, they drank too much, they engaged in violent love affairs, they fell ill.

I would have thought that I would be no good at all at the job of looking after them – no self-confidence, rather nervous, easily hurt, not very brave. But I couldn't put a foot wrong. All the time I had the feeling I was being helped to do and say the right thing. I loved them all so much I hadn't time to be 'hurt in my feelings', or to wonder if they loved me, or to be afraid of driving on icy roads, giving them hell if they misbehaved, arguing their cases with Austrian officials. All the time it seemed that God was there, and in a way this bothered me, because I have never believed in a god who can, so to speak, tell me, from 'without' or 'beyond' what to do – I should have said, too, that I didn't believe in prayer as I understood it. But I prayed for those young people; that is, I thought about them, pitied them, and hoped for them until it hurt – physically.

This was the first of such experiences: it gave me confidence and courage, and increased my capacity to love. It also put me in a dilemma: whether or not to accept a nine-months' job helping in the resettlement of refugees, and to delay by that period rejoining my husband. It didn't 'feel' right to take the job, but perhaps it would be shirking to refuse. In the end I spoke to a priest about it, a priest who preached often about service to the unfortunate and involvement with one's neighbour. He said I should go to my husband, that wherever I was I should find work to do if I looked for it. He was perfectly right. I was asked to take charge of the adult literacy programme in a 700-bed government hospital in Africa. I had to learn the language properly, find helpers, organize a rota and transport, and spend every afternoon from 1.30–4 at the hospital. Most helpers could give only one afternoon a week, some only one a fortnight: whatever they couldn't do I tried to do. We worked mostly in the surgical wards and during the hottest time of the day. It was extremely tiring, and often the wards smelled awful. But I found myself going as though to a party and coming away as exhilarated as if I'd had a good stiff drink. I've never met such wonderful people: patient, enduring, cheerful, eager to learn, and incredibly brave. Their love was an honour and a benediction, and again I felt I walked with God, even though I rejected the image of somebody 'up there' putting out a hand to me. When I had time to think about it I used to wonder if I were becoming what one might call a love-addict, the kind of person who will do anything to win love, and who goes about the place behaving as though she thought she was a mixture of the Lady with the Lamp and Napoleon! You know the sort? But nobody around me seemed to think so: my husband and children would never have let me get away with it if *they* had noticed. So I gave up fussing and just worked on till we left Africa. I prayed for those people as I had done for my Hungarian sons and daughters and wept to leave them all.

After we came back my mother died. She left me some money, and after a great deal of thought I've decided what to do with it. I am to foster, and in a year or two we may be allowed to adopt, an English-Jamaican baby. He is now seven months old and will come to us next month if all goes well. He has nobody: if we don't take him he'll go into an institution. The family agrees – my children enthusiastically and my husband because he loves me. Often I'm terrified when I think what I'm taking on, and if it hadn't been for Austria and Africa I shouldn't be grown up enough to have considered it. Fundamentally, however, I'm not afraid. I know I can bring him up, love him, and keep him out of my husband's hair! It is a job to last me till I die. I think it must be right, or I wouldn't be so happy. In prospect, at any rate, it isn't narrowing: all sorts of people seem nicer and more lovable because of this small coffee-coloured child!

I have told you these things because your book – which I might not have read if I hadn't heard what you said about radicalism on the BBC – has made clearer to me *why* I think and act as I do, why the last few years have been years of growth and change and happiness. It has made many things fall into place in my mind and helped me to understand myself as I used to be and am now. I used, I think, to look for God when I was miserable, or felt inadequate and unloved. ('Nobody loves me and my hands are cold' – 'God loves you and you can sit on your hands!'). I didn't find him because he wasn't there, and I had the brains to recognize this and to learn to do without him. And then, when I was too busy to think and worry about myself, there he seemed to be. But I was too conditioned by an agnostic background – 'agnostic', be it said, in the true Greek sense of the word – to turn round and believe in 'that gentleman who's always there' (as the small boy complained!). So I just shelved the problem, because I was too ignorant to know that better and cleverer people had spent and were spending their time and thought on it. That is why I thank you most earnestly for your book, for explaining what you and they have made of it, have pondered and written about the nature of God.

There are parts of the creeds I can't say. I don't see how I could honestly be confirmed. I don't know of any church where communion is celebrated in the spirit you describe. I am sure that Jesus is the son of God but am obscurely comforted by the NEB's 'beloved' instead of 'only'. I don't know whether I have the right to have my little foster child baptized. '*Wherein* I was made, etc.', sticks in my gullet. Are the Tibetan children and the Moslems I love not children of God and inheritors of the Kingdom of Heaven? I don't understand the Resurrection as any churchman I know seems to. But Matt. 22.37–40 [Jesus' summary of the Law as love of God and neighbour] has meant increasingly much to me for a long time, and I think you have shown me why. Is it because those words are the core of the matter and so enough?

> If this is a gross oversimplification of what you have written, I'm sorry: misdirected thanks are worse than none, and yet I wouldn't dare to ask you to argue with me or try to correct me. So this letter must stand, as the best explanation and expression of my gratitude that I can give.

A woman of twenty, an undergraduate at Oxford, wrote:

> Many prominent men in the Church of England have allowed their unmeditated reaction to your ideas to appear in print. Such men are unaware of the urgency of the need for a new image, and of the harmful contempt for the Christian religion which the old mythological image arouses amongst the younger generation, both at university and in the ordinary grammar school.
>
> The C. S. Lewis type argument, which is so popular amongst teachers and progressive Bible study group leaders, only alienates this youth further. They turn to Eastern religions, but practice is difficult and soon interest fades. Eventually they enter the rat race after 'O' or 'A' levels, diplomas or degree, without committing themselves positively to a particular way of living their lives.
>
> Large numbers of us do not want to throw out our Christian heritage (if that were possible) because it stresses the importance of respect for the rights of the individual, which is closely linked with political and civil freedom.
>
> I would like to tell you that your radical reinterpretation is just what is needed to make Christian religion *dynamic* and *viable*. Overnight it has been reinfused with life, and tremendous power unleashed.

A woman of eighty-three, presumably interested in more than 'the rights of the individual', wrote: 'Although a fairly regular church attender I have for many years been full of inward doubts and questionings. Your book has answered them and for my short remaining time on this earth I shall be more at peace and more ready to cope with life and its many contacts. Thank you, and again thank you.' A number of other old people wrote in similar terms.

II

Honest to God Now

The Flowering of Honesty

Eric James

I first got to know Bishop John Robinson – 'Honest John', as some came to call him – thirty-six years ago, when he was Dean of Clare College, Cambridge, and I was Chaplain of Trinity.

John had heard that I loved his uncle Forbes' book *Letters to his Friends*, which had been privately printed in 1904, and had sold over 12,000 copies. John asked me whether I'd be willing to prepare a new edition of the book. Most of the correspondents in the original edition were only referred to by their initials, and John thought the time had come for their anonymity to be ended. He thought it might be good to give a paragraph of biography to each of the thirty correspondents, and also a biographical sketch of the author, who had been Dean of Christ's College, Cambridge, when he wrote the letters, but had died of tuberculosis at only thirty-seven.

I learnt from that first encounter how much the family John had been born into meant to him. He was forever digging into his roots – *The Roots of a Radical* – as he was to call one of his last books, published in 1980. 'For a radical,' he wrote, 'has to be a person of roots and deep roots: with the freedom and courage, as Jesus did, to go to the source and speak from the centre.' 'Roots,' John maintained, 'are neither for boasting, nor for despising.' He wanted to be honest about Forbes Robinson as part of being honest to himself.

John knew in his bones that honesty was an essential virtue for the person who belonged to the church in the world today. As I got to know him – and his wife and family – I began to see him as a man who was intent on relating the church to the world with a rigorous honesty.

A Cambridge college chapel might not seem very close to the world, but two of John's first books – *The Body* and *Liturgy Coming to Life* – are honest testimony to a kind of conversion. John had come to see that salvation is not to be sought by withdrawing from the collectives of modern society and by exalting the individual, but by personal life lived in solidarity with others – like those whose lives he had shared as a curate in the slums of Bristol, and those in the Cambridge college of which he was the Dean.

Mervyn Stockwood – to whom John had been curate in Bristol – persuaded him to be his assistant Bishop of Southwark. So on 29 September, Michaelmas Day, 1959, John was consecrated Bishop of Woolwich. Five days later, he was present at my induction as Vicar of St George's, Camberwell, which was in his part of the Diocese of Southwark, South London. So, having been close to him in Cambridge, I was also close to John all the years he was Bishop of Woolwich, and was able to see at first hand what his honesty drove him to do and be.

His first major effort at honest realism as a bishop was the founding of the Southwark Ordination Course. It was to be a theological college without walls. By the end of 1961, just two years after his consecration, this pioneer training scheme for people in secular employment began. In June 1960 I had heard John give a talk at a conference in Oxford on what he called 'Taking the lid off the church's ministry'. He wanted to break down the barriers, he said, between those who got paid for their ministry and lived off it and those who would be ordained but continue in their secular work; the barriers between clergy and laity, and between men in the ministry and women.

John wasn't only honest about his views on the church's ministry. He also spoke in the Convocation of Canterbury in January 1961 against capital punishment and on 'Ought Suicide to be a Crime?'

But it must be said that the stir John caused in Convocation was in large part due to the explosion which he had caused some months before, in October 1960, by declaring openly and honestly what he felt about the publication of an unexpurgated edition of D. H. Lawrence's *Lady Chatterley's Lover*.

The 25 August 1960 was the seventy-fifth anniversary of D. H. Lawrence's birth and the thirtieth of his death, and Penguin Books had prepared the unexpurgated edition as a celebration. John had been invited to appear as a witness for the defence in proceedings under the Obscene Publications Act. It took him only three days to make up his mind whether he was in favour of supporting the publication, and whether, as a bishop of the church of God, he should speak in the book's defence.

At the beginning of the case, Mr Justice Byrne decided the jury should read the book in a special room within the Old Bailey. Mr Griffith-Jones then opened for the prosecution, and on 27 October 1960, Mr Gerald Gardiner, QC, later a distinguished Lord Chancellor, opened the case for the defence.

John was only one of more than thirty witnesses for the defence – like E. M. Forster, Roy Jenkins, and C. Day-Lewis. He soon found himself strenuously maintaining that the book was against rather than for sexual promiscuity. In the closing speech for the defence, Gerald Gardiner reminded the jury of John's words: 'Clearly Lawrence did not have a Christian valuation of sex, and the kind of sexual relationship depicted in the book is not one that I would necessarily regard as ideal, but what I think is clear is that what Lawrence is trying to do is to portray the sex relationship as something essentially sacred.'

It was the Bishop of Woolwich's evidence that everyone remembered. His answers supplied the banner headlines for the evening papers: 'Christians should read Lady C'. 'Bishop: Essentially something sacred'.

If it was John's evidence people remembered, what they also remembered was the question Mr Griffith-Jones had asked within the first hour of the first day of the trial: 'Is it a book that you would even wish your wife and your servants to read?' That question made it clear that the trial was crucial not simply concerning what constitutes literary merit and what does not, but as something that marked out, to use the phrase of Bernard Levin, *The Pendulum Years*. Mr Griffith-Jones belonged to one era – and, indeed, to one way of life; those who spoke in support of the publication of the unexpurgated edition of *Lady Chetterley* belonged to another.

The decade which began with the prosecution of Penguin Books for publishing *Lady Chatterley's Lover* had seen, before it ended, with no prosecution or threat of it, the publication of books such as Philip Roth's *Portnoy's Complaint*, William Burroughs' *The Naked Truth* and a number of others which it is fairly safe to say would have been very lucky to escape conviction if they and not Lawrence's work had been the subject of the 'test case' in 1960. Some, of course, saw what was accomplished only as ruin and corruption; others believed a healthy freedom of expression had been established. A decade or so later, Philip Larkin, looking back, memorably summed up the mood of the Sixties – and of the freedom achieved – in his poem 'Annus Mirabilis':

> Sexual intercourse began
> In nineteen sixty-three
> (Which was rather late for me) –
> Between the end of the *Chatterley* ban
> And the Beatles' first LP.[1]

Of course, there were other signs of the times. With the Beatles appeared the Maharishi. There was the Profumo Case, which nearly destroyed the Prime Minister, Harold Macmillan – and his government – but brought Lord Denning and his Report to everyone's lips. *Lady Chatterley* – charged and acquitted – survived and did more than survive: Lawrence's one unpublished and unpublishable book soon sold several million copies.

But to return to John Robinson. Two days after the end of the 'trial', the then Archbishop of Canterbury, Geoffrey Fisher, at his Diocesan Conference publicly censured John. 'In my judgment,' the Archbishop said, 'the Bishop was mistaken to think that he could take part in this trial without becoming a stumbling block and a cause of offence to many ordinary Christians.'

John defended himself in the next Sunday's *Observer*. He said he had no regrets whatever for his part in what he called 'this crucial case' – crucial for the exposure of hypocrisy on the subject of obscene publications.

The next story over John's honesty arose from the publication of *Honest to God* in March 1963.

Re-reading *Honest to God* now, it is quite difficult to see what all the fuss was about. In part, it was the headline which was given to an article in *The Observer*, which acted as a curtain-raiser the Sunday before the book's publication: 'Our Image of God must Go'.

That headline had been provided by *The Observer*. When it was suggested, it struck John as negative and arrogant, and he resisted it, but under pressure of time, he eventually concurred. But a headline could not of itself have accounted for the 4,000 letters John received, the TV programmes, broadcasts, cartoons, articles, reviews and sermons. *Honest to God* sold out its first impression on the day of publication. Bowler-hatted men queued for copies on Waterloo station. It sold well over a million copies and was translated into seventeen languages.

Beside *The Observer* headline, there was also the powerful cover-photograph of the book: the German sculptor Wilhelm Lehmbruck's 'Seated Youth 1918', reminiscent of Rodin's 'Thinker'. And, of course, there was the title – *Honest to God* – which was in fact suggested by Ruth, John's wife. John himself at first thought it too flippant, but David Edwards, then head of SCM Press, the publishers, said 'That's it!' And it was. It was the title which undoubtedly made a major contribution to the book's success.

The mood of the book – which spoke to the world of the sixties – is probably best conveyed by an article John wrote for the *Sunday Mirror* in April 1963 less than three weeks after the publication of the book.

> What drove me to write my book was that what matters to ... most people in life seems to have nothing to do with 'God'; and God has no connection with what really concerns them day by day.
>
> At best he seems to come in only at the edges of life. He is out there somewhere as a sort of long-stop – at death, or to

turn to in tragedy (either to pray to or to blame).

The traditional imagery of God simply succeeds, I believe, in making him remote for millions today.

What I want to do is not to deny God in any sense, but to put him back into the middle of life – where Jesus showed us he belongs.

For the Christian God is not remote. He is involved; he is implicated. If Jesus Christ means anything, he means that God belongs to this world.

So let's start not from a heavenly Being, whose very existence many would doubt. Let's start from what actually is most real to people in everyday life – and find God there.[2]

As with *Lady Chatterley*, so with *Honest to God*: again John was censured by the Archbishop of Canterbury – this time in an interview on television. It particularly hurt John, for the Archbishop was now the scholar, Michael Ramsey, whom he greatly respected. It was 1 April 1963 when the Archbishop appeared on television. On 2 April John wrote a letter to the Archbishop:

I really am distressed that you should seriously suppose that I am unaware of the pastoral problem concerned. I am acutely conscious of it, and if we had met I would have hoped to convince you of this before you spoke in public. It is of course utterly untrue to say that I wish to 'denounce the imagery of God held by Christian men and women and children' or to say that 'we can't have any new thought until it is all swept away'. I thought I had made this clear in my book time and again. It will be enough to quote from page forty-three, in which I condemn any such denunciatory language: 'To speak thus one is in danger, like the Psalmist, of condemning a whole generation – indeed many, many generations – of God's children. It is still the language of most of his children – and particularly his older children. There is nothing intrinsically wrong with it, any more than there was with the symbolism of a localized heaven. There will be many – and indeed most of us most of the time – for whom it presents no serious difficulties and no insuperable barriers to belief.' Indeed, the very title of my first chapter 'Reluctant Revolution' was intended to convey – as it is clear that the whole book has conveyed to any sympathetic reader – that this was an agony in which I found myself just as much on one side as the other. So far from writing off those who accept the traditional framework, I do so with a large part of myself.

Perhaps I may quote the impression it made on Canon Max Warren, who writes in the Southwark Diocesan Review: 'This is a *gentle* book. That may seem a curious adjective to use about one of the hardest hitting books the reader is likely to have met. Yet Dr Robinson remains all the time very gentle, very sensitive not only to those whom he is trying to reach, but also to those Christians who will find his approach very disconcerting and puzzling and who will not be able to follow him . . .' At least my book seems to have touched people at a point where truth really matters to them. And of this I am glad – even if it has inevitably meant some pain. For it is at this point that God may be able to become real for them again.

I am sorry to have written at such length. I would much rather have talked. As you know, I offered to let you see the manuscript last summer, and nothing would please me more than to feel that (even if we disagree theologically) at least I had your understanding. I am grieved that fellowship between bishops should be reduced to exchanges on television and in the popular press. This is another part of the pastoral situation that gives me concern.

John did not lose any time in thinking out how to use *Honest to God*, particularly in the Diocese of Southwark. He visited the sixth forms of schools, and, of course, churches, and held a series of conferences to follow up his book. Curiously, despite the usual tendency of the media to fasten on morals, the chapter in *Honest to God* headed 'The New Morality' provided virtually no controversy at all. Then suddenly morals were at the eye of the storm.

Two years earlier, John had promised the then Bishop of Liverpool, Clifford Martin, to deliver three lectures on Christian ethics, in Liverpool Cathedral, at the end of October 1963. First published as *Christian Morals Today*, they were models of careful thinking and writing.

> At the expense of being fundamental rather than quotable, I want to try to dig down a bit, to see if we cannot establish some mutual confidence and common ground ...
>
> I am deeply concerned that at this juncture there shall be a real attempt at mutual understanding and communication. For I believe that the 'old' and the 'new' morality ... corresponding with two starting-points, two approaches to certain perennial polarities in Christian ethics ... or really it is the same polarity under three aspects. The first is that between the elements of fixity and freedom, the second that between law and love, and the third that between authority and experience.
>
> The first of these is thrust upon our attention at once by the overall title chosen for these lectures – 'Christian Morals *Today*'. In what sense are Christian morals today different from Christian morals yesterday? Is there not an abiding Christian ethic? Indeed, can you have a new morality any more than a new gospel? The tension here is between the constant and the variable, the absolute and the relative, the eternal and the changing.
>
> Now, neither side in the present controversy, I would submit, has any interest in denying either of these complementary elements ... The 'new morality' is not in the least interested in jettisoning law, or in weakening what in *Honest to God* I called 'the dykes of love in a loveless world'. But it also believes it has something to say which is not an incitement to immorality or to individualism, and for which it craves a quiet, unemotional and honest hearing.[3]

John protested in vain. He was now to his enemies the high priest of the Permissive Society.

John's honesty was displayed in a kind of three-pronged trident: honesty in Christian doctrine, honesty concerning sexual ethics, and honesty relating to the pastoral situation of the church. His lectures in the United States published in 1965 as *The New Reformation?* were a good example of the latter.

John's output was astonishing. He was, for instance, a regular contributor to the journal *New Christian* which had its first edition in October 1961. In 1967 his *Exploration into God* was published – the much respected Jesuit philosopher, F. C. Coppleston, had written:

> By publishing *Honest to God* the bishop won for himself an extremely wide circle of readers. He succeeded in shocking or startling many people into thinking and talking about theological matters. If therefore he could write for his public, in similarly popular style, a book exhibiting more positively and fully the foundations of his Christian vision of reality, he might do a tremendous amount of good. Perhaps this is an impertinent suggestion to make. But it seems to me that the Bishop of Woolwich is faced with an opportunity which rarely comes to anyone in his position.[4]

John was unlikely to fail to respond to an invitation and challenge like that. And *Exploration into God* was undoubtedly one of John's best books. It was unashamedly autobiographical.

> All my deepest concerns both in thought and in action – and I cannot separate the theological, the pastoral and the political – find their centre in a single, continuing quest. This is to give expression, embodiment, to the overmastering, yet elusive, conviction of the 'Thou' at the heart of everything. It is a quest for the form of the personal as the ultimate reality in life, as the deepest truth about all one's relationships and commitments. How can one give shape to the conviction that the personal is the controlling category for the interpretation of everything, both conceptually and in action? That it is this is one of those basic acts of trust of which it is impossible to say whether it comes from one's Christian commitment or whether Christianity authenticates itself because it provides its definition and vindication. At any rate it is, as near as I can determine it, my central concern, that which chiefly decides what rings a bell, what I respond to as meaningful, significant, stimulating.[5]

Exploration into God undoubtedly cleared up much that John had left unclear in *Honest to God*.

John Robinson's years as Bishop of Woolwich were ten punishing years – not least physically. He suffered fairly continuously from back trouble. So when it was suggested to him that he had a *magnum opus* in him on christology, but that he would only really be able to write it at a university, when he was invited to be Dean of Trinity College, Cambridge, and to give the Hulsean Lectures, he accepted, and soon got down to writing the lectures – published as *The Human Face of God*, in 1973.

Although his years as Dean of Trinity enabled him to lecture all round the globe, they were always to some extent an anticlimax after Southwark. There was the feeling that the Church of England had not killed its prophet, but it had relatively speaking, silenced him, by prevailing upon him to take an academic position – and to offer him no other post in fourteen years.

And then came the end. In the Easter Term in 1983 it became apparent that John was terminally ill – with cancer of the pancreas. He died six months to the day after his surgeon had spoken to him of his having six more months of life. But the way he lived those last six months was itself a revelation of John's honesty – to God and to the world.

At his request, I sat next to him, in Trinity College Chapel, when, on 23 October 1983, he preached his last sermon 'On Learning from Cancer'. All that sermon is worthy of quotation as an example of his honesty. But a few sentences must now suffice:

> 'Human kind', said Eliot, 'cannot bear very much reality.' It is difficult for me to comprehend that there are people who just do not want to know whether they have got cancer. But above all there is a conspiracy of silence ostensibly to protect others. We think they cannot face it, though in my experience they usually know deep down; and obviously it is critical how they are told and who tells them (and of course whether they really need to know). But what we are much more likely to be doing is mutually protecting ourselves ... For we dare not

face it in ourselves or talk about it at the levels of reality that we might open up.

But Christians above all are those who should be able to bear reality and show others how to bear it. Or what are we to say about the cross, the central reality of our faith? ...

Healing cannot be confined to any, or indeed every, level of human understanding or expectation. This is why too it shows up those twin deceivers pessimism and optimism as so shallow. In the course of nature, cancer-sufferers swing from one to the other more than most, as good days and bad days, remissions and recurrences, follow each other. But the Christian takes his stand not on optimism but on hope. This is based not on rosy prognosis (from the human point of view mine is bleak) but, as St Paul says, on suffering. For this, he says, trains us to endure and endurance brings proof that we have stood the tests, and this proof is the ground of hope – in the God who can bring resurrection out and through the other side of death.[6]

Life was Never the Same

Ruth Robinson

When I made the remark which gives this programme its title I was answering a question about how the publication of *Honest to God* affected our own household. But it was also true, in one sense, of the religious scene. Questions were raised openly in the book which would never again go away.

Yet, looking back over thirty years, I have to say that I do not think the implications of some of those questions were always fully realized or honestly followed through. On the religious front, traditional positions have become more entrenched and unyielding. People can ask with some justification: 'Whatever happened to *Honest to God*?' Has that tide of interest in religion just drained away into the sand? Or is it that, like Joanna Trollope's *Rector's Wife*, we have given up expecting to find answers to our questions in the church?

> Anxiously, Anna had sometimes wondered if Peter (her husband) had lost his faith. As for herself, she was uncertain she had ever had any, and yet, for all that, she sometimes joyfully felt that she knew what it was about. She had tried to explain this fleeting instinctive comprehension to Peter, but he had said, 'I think you are confusing faith with emotion', so she had not tried again.[1]

But perhaps it was Peter, the vicar, who was confusing belief with vision. It is time to put in a word for that 'fleeting instinctive comprehension' and to set belief in perspective.

Religious beliefs are human constructions. Ideas of God, as

creator or father, are human ideas. Language about God gives no information about anyone other than ourselves. It speaks only about our experience of the world and our response to it. This acknowledgment is in no way to 'rubbish' God language. On the contrary, it means we can take it seriously. Belief statements are metaphors. They build up the story framework we invent to communicate a shared inner vision.

It is difficult to disentangle how much of the Christian vision originated from Jesus himself and how much from those who intuitively responded to him. But at the heart of their perception was a corporate experience, after the death of Jesus, of a powerful compassionate energy which had completely transformed them.

They described what had happened to them in the language of their own cosmology, in the story of God sending his own Son into the world because he loved it. This indeed came as Good News, especially to the poor, the disabled and the exploited, whose lives were ruled by arbitrary powers over which they had no control.

This story has been told through succeeding generations and something of the original vision continues to break through. But the further we get from its source, the more it appears that the emphasis shifted.

The details of the story gained more and more factual significance, even ones introduced later to stress a theological point, like the old myth of a virgin birth, or, later still, theories of original sin and of God as a Trinity of three persons.

By the fifth century, an official version of the story was established, outside which any shared understanding of the original version was unacceptable and even condemned. For many people now, literal belief in this official version strangles the vision.

Richard Bach tells this fable in his book *Illusions: The Adventures of a Reluctant Messiah.*

Once there lived a village of creatures along the bottom of a great crystal river.

The current of the river swept silently over them all – young and old, rich and poor, good and evil, the current going its own way, knowing only its own crystal self.

Each creature in its own manner clung tightly to the twigs and rocks of the river bottom, for clinging was their way of life, and resisting the current what each had learned from birth.

But one creature said at last, 'I'm tired of clinging. Though I cannot see it with my eyes, I trust that the current knows where it is going. I shall let go, and let it take me where it will. Clinging, I shall die of boredom.'

The other creatures laughed and said, 'Fool! Let go, and that current you worship will throw you tumbled and smashed across the rocks, and you will die quicker than by boredom!'

But the one heeded them not, and taking a breath did let go, and at once was tumbled and smashed by the current across the rocks.

Yet in time, as the creature refused to cling again, the current lifted him free from the bottom, and he was bruised and hurt no more.

And the creatures downstream, to whom he was a stranger, cried, 'See a miracle! A creature like ourselves, yet he flies! See the Messiah, come to save us all!'

And the one carried in the current said, 'I am no more Messiah than you. The river delights to lift us free, if only we dare let go. Our true work is this voyage, this adventure.'

But they cried the more, 'Saviour!', all the while clinging to the rocks, and when they looked again he was gone, and they were left alone making legends of a Saviour.[2]

While the churches cling to beliefs that many cannot share, the world is lost without a vision. Economic growth and material wealth is as far as we can see. Our attention is increasingly drawn to the trivial and the commonplace. We are losing our crafting skills. The jobless are undervalued. Many feel worthless and become apathetic or violent.

The churches did once supply a vision to live by. Today, with notable exceptions, their inward-looking preoccupations and banal services are losing credibility. Where there is vitality it is often associated with an evangelistic fervour which can easily exploit guilt, fear and loneliness.

We can't afford to ignore the threat of exclusive belief too insistently held. Non-believers can quickly become enemies and religious wars a fanatical obligation. All religions are vulnerable to this ominous degeneration when believing a doctrine becomes more important than trusting a vision.

It was William Blake, that great visionary, who invented the aphorism: 'The cistern contains; the fountain overflows.' Official Christianity is trying to contain an original vision in a belief system which is becoming rusty and springing leaks. It can't be done. That vision produced a fountain of creative energy that can't be domesticated for church use only. The overflowing source is there for all.

In all religions there have been those who have followed an inner vision and who have enlightened our understanding and transformed us by their imaginative perception.

The old Persian poets and Sufis of Islam, the Zen masters of Buddhism, the Vedantic writers of Hinduism, Old Testament prophets and poets, Jewish and Christian mystics, all have fired the human imagination and made us more aware of the vision that lies behind creed and doctrine.

Even the Church Fathers who formulated the Christian creeds seemed to hint at hidden mysteries, a 'secret doctrine' not publicly divulged but kept for initiates who could understand the inner meaning.

Theologians now do not interpret the creeds literally, but in church we are asked to affirm them as if we do.

These two streams of tradition, visionary and credal, have always been there. Sadly, established religion has too often clung to credal statement and marginalized the visionary, even to denouncing it as heresy. And so a large part of our Christian tradition has been unacknowledged. And, with it too, the substratum of female spirituality unacknowledged.

It is time to claim our full inheritance and to affirm that tradition is not fixed in the past but is a living, flowing process into which our own understanding is gathered. One creed maker of the fourth century suggested for example that the Holy Spirit was only becoming clear in the life of the church. There is no reason to suppose that this process stopped in the fifth century. Edward Robinson, John's brother, says in his book *The Language of Mystery*:

> No human society can prosper without tradition, but tradition if it is to be kept in good heart needs constantly to be rescued from those who would preserve it from change ... if it is to be kept in good health it must be by a continuous process of organic renewal.
>
> (We should not) be ungrateful to those who love their tradition and try to prevent its dissolution. But too possessive a care for its preservation can, as we know, lead its self-appointed guardians to cut off those very energies by which it can be revitalized.[3]

Religious belief was at home in a three-decker universe, where the comings and goings between heaven, earth and hell could be easily visualized. It could also fit comfortably in a Newtonian universe, where everything worked like clockwork, and God could be imagined starting it off, keeping it in order and making sure everything worked out for the best.

With the appearance of quantum physics 'life was never the same'. Most of us are only dimly aware of all it means, and scientists have as much difficulty in making us understand what a black hole is as theologians had in explaining the Trinity. Physicists too have become visionaries, stretching language to convey paradox and ambiguity. They too work with mystery. Einstein himself is quoted as saying: 'The most beautiful experience we can have is the mysterious. It is the fundamental emotion that stands at the cradle of true art and true science. Whoever does not know it and can no longer wonder, no longer marvel, is as good as dead.'

Now we live in a universe where nothing can be understood except in relation to everything else, where simply observing changes what happens, where time only seems to move forwards. We can no longer think of ourselves as separate from nature. The same patterns are found in the nerves of the retina and in wave movements on the beach. One single atom of iron instead of one of magnesium is all the difference between blood and chlorophyll. We are as one organism.

In such a universe, mystics and visionaries speak to us with an authentic voice. Hildegard of Bingen in the twelfth century talked of God's moistness and greening power and of Christ's bringing 'lush greenness' to 'shrivelled and wilted' people and institutions.

> I am the breeze that nurtures all things green.
> I encourage blossoms to flourish with ripening fruits,
> I am the rain coming from the dew
> that causes the grasses to laugh
> with the joy of life.[4]

The physicist David Bohm describes the universe as an implicate order in which every element contains enfolded within itself the totality of the whole. Julian of Norwich imagined a little thing as small as a hazelnut in the palm of her hand and saw that it was all that is made. William Blake saw heaven in a grain of sand.

Intuition and imagination play a significant part in science. And religion too is an imaginative exploration. We undertake it because we choose to look for meaning, we want to express reverence, to acknowledge wonder and celebrate delight.

It is our poets, artists and musicians who speak what Edward Robinson calls 'the language of mystery'. They help us to see and to listen. They are our priests and our celebrants. The Greek poet Seferis describes a poet as 'one who creates sacramental relationship'.

Poets and artists heighten our perception, giving us a keener vision and recording for us what we have no power to say ourselves. Like John Steinbeck in *East of Eden*, they speak for everyone.

> Sometimes a kind of glory lights up the mind of a man. It happens to nearly everyone. You can feel it growing or preparing like a fuse burning towards dynamite. It is a feeling in the stomach, a delight of the nerves, of the forearms. The skin tastes the air, and every deep-drawn breath is sweet. Its

> beginning has the pleasure of a great stretching yawn; it flashes in the brain and the whole world glows outside your eyes. A man may have lived all of his life in the grey, and the land and trees of him dark and sombre. The events, even the important ones, may have trooped by, faceless and pale. And then – the glory – so that a cricket song sweetens his ears, the smell of the earth rises chanting to his nose, and dappling light under a tree blesses his eyes. Then a man pours outward, a torrent of him, and yet he is not diminished.[5]

'If the glory can be killed,' John Steinbeck says, 'we are lost.' Art keeps it alive, by word and sight and sound.

We cannot simply be observers. In a concert, the music needs our listening. The relationship is two-way. The world too waits for our response and comes to us as Presence as in Kathleen Raine's poem called 'The Presence'.

> Present, ever-present presence,
> Never have you not been
> Here and now in every now and here,
> And still you bring
> From your treasury of colour, of light,
> Of scents, of notes, the evening blackbird's song,
> How clear among the green and fragrant leaves,
> As in childhood always new, anew.
> My hand that writes is ageing, but I too
> Repeat only and again
> The one human song, from memory
> Of a joy, a mode
> Not I but the music knows
> That forms, informs us, utters without voices
> Concord of heaven and earth, of high and low, who are
> That music of the spheres Pythagoras heard.
> I, living, utter as the blackbird
> In ignorance of what it tells, the undying voice.[6]

The experience of glory or Presence is part of an inner discovery. We each have to find our own way but take with us what is precious to us from our own tradition.

I am one of those who start from the Christian tradition, but

I don't carry with me all the proper credentials.

I don't believe the Bible is the Word of God. It is a human, though almost exclusively male, story of how one patriarchal tribe found its identity as a nation. Its heroes are men and women who are often victims of the God their tradition has invented. But it is a compilation of folk-tale, history and vision, full of marvellous poetry, insight and wisdom.

I don't believe in a Father in Heaven who sent his Son to live as a man. Or that this Son's cruel death was necessary to cancel out all human sin. But I know that love requires us to forgive each other and sometimes to die for each other, and be forgiven, and that both are costly.

I don't know what happened to the body of Jesus, but I know that where there is love, death and loss can release a new energy.

I don't believe that Jesus was *uniquely* different from other human beings, or that his is the *only* self-sacrifice that matters. I don't *know* that he loved more than anyone else has loved, or that he is the *only* one to have experienced God with such intimacy. As Jung said: 'What happens in the life of Christ happens always and everywhere.'

The real story is more than a record of events that happened two thousand years ago. It is the drama of being human. We are the story, and we make it happen.

Meister Eckhart knew this in the thirteenth century. In a Christmas sermon he said:

> Here in time we make holiday because the eternal birth which God the Father bore and bears unceasingly in eternity is now born in time, in human nature. St Augustine says that birth is always happening. But if it happen not in me what does it profit me? What matter is that it shall happen in me.[7]

Blake knew it in his vision of Divine Humanity.

> For Mercy has a human heart,
> Pity, a human face,
> And Love, the human form divine,
> And Peace, the human dress.

Then every man of every clime
That prays in his distress
Prays to the human form divine,
Love Mercy Pity Peace.

And all must love the human form
In heathen, turk or jew.
Where Mercy, Love and Pity dwell
There God is dwelling too.[8]

God is not separate from humanity. We are responsible for doing the God-work. Christ is the true Self in each of us and in each other. Human compassion and self-giving love is able to transform the world. That is the Christian hope.

Jesus articulated and focussed this vision. It required a shift of consciousness which must happen in us too. He forced us to look at things differently, and life was never the same again.

I want to end with two pictures. One is Thomas Traherne's vision of the world seen through the eyes of a child; the other an image of a London childhood today.

> The corn was orient and immortal wheat, which never should be reaped, nor was ever sown. I thought it had stood from everlasting to everlasting. The dust and stones of the street were as precious as gold; the gates were at first the end of the world. The green trees when I saw them first through one of the gates transported and ravished me, their sweetness and unusual beauty made my heart to leap, and almost mad with ecstasy, they were such strange and wonderful things. The Men! O what venerable and reverend creatures did the aged seem! Immortal Cherubims! And young men glittering and sparkling Angels, and maids strange seraphic pieces of life and beauty! Boys and girls, tumbling in the street, and playing, were moving jewels. I knew not that they were born or should die; but all things abided eternally as they were in their proper places. Eternity was manifest in the Light of the Day, and something infinite behind everything appeared: which talked with my expectation and moved my desire. The city seemed

> to stand in Eden, or to be built in Heaven. The streets were mine, the temple was mine, the people were mine, their clothes and gold and silver were mine, as much as their sparkling eyes, fair skins and ruddy faces. The skies were mine, and so were the sun and moon and stars, and all the World was mine; and I the only spectator and I enjoyer of it. I knew no churlish properties, nor bounds, nor divisions: but all properties and divisions were mine: all treasures and the possessors of them. So that with much ado I was corrupted, and made to learn the dirty devices of this world. Which now I unlearn, and become, as it were, a little child again that I may enter into the Kingdom of God.[9]

Just before New Year I was returning home across London after a Christmas visit. On an underground stairway a small thin boy was huddled in a corner. His face was grey and his eyes looked desperate and hopeless. A piece of cardboard was lying on the ground beside him. Among the pennies scattered on it two words were written: 'Change please'.

The child was asking only for money. How could *he* see the world as Traherne once saw it, or hope for such a change in his? But nothing less than this is enough. The Kingdom of God is a vision of our world transformed. To enter it we must unlearn the dirty devices of cynicism, apathy, greed. The love of God is a vision of the human heart transformed, by compassion, hope and trust. We change the world by loving it for the sake of every child.

Without a compassionate vision we are dead. We must trust it enough to follow where it leads.

A Loss of Nerve

John Bowden

'He may well lose his job.' That was my first introduction to *Honest to God.* I was curate of a city church in Nottingham in March 1963 and had been invited up to the university one Saturday night to hear David Edwards of SCM Press talking about a sensational new book which was about to burst on the world. 'Read *The Observer* tomorrow,' he told us, and there it was: a banner headline right across the review section, 'Our Image of God Must Go.' Next morning I was down at the local bookshop the moment it opened, persuading the friendly assistant to let me buy, the day before publication, one of the select 6,000 copies of the first printing. Others had to wait for one of the countless reprints which came that year.

Of course John Robinson didn't lose his job because of *Honest to God.* And I might have taken David Edwards' words with a large pinch of salt had I known what his biographer subsequently revealed: there had been considerable consultation before the manuscript had been accepted and a copy had even been sent to the Archbishop of Canterbury. (He had had no time to read it but sent good wishes.) But there was a sensation.

I read the book immediately, and – to be as honest as its author tried to be – I wasn't bowled over. To those who had been at certain Anglican theological colleges at the end of the 1950s, the ideas expressed in *Honest to God* weren't new: we had already revelled in the thought of Bonhoeffer, Bultmann and Tillich, the German theologians who provided much of the dynamite for John Robinson's bombshell, and in even more explosive works that he hadn't read. For questioning young theologians he was already behind the times. After all, he was quoting from classics all of which had been published at least ten years earlier. The difference was that he had got everyone talking about God – on radio and TV, in the national newspapers, in the pubs and round my parish. Somehow he had put together these disparate theologians and much else in one small paperback, in a heady mix. And he was a bishop. So like many others, while I brashly found his book almost old-fashioned as well as ambiguous, I was firmly on his side, in the hope that something new and revolutionary might actually be about to happen in the churches.

We now know that it didn't, and doesn't seem very likely to. I succeeded David Edwards as Editor and Managing Director of SCM Press, and am still there now, and one of the things I have to live with is that, thirty years after *Honest to God* (and despite recent much-publicized moves, like the Church of England's decision to ordain women priests), the churches have become more and more reactionary. It's worth asking why, especially as many of the answers lie in John Robinson and his book.

I wouldn't want anything I say to obscure my enormous admiration for John Robinson's achievements. Our characters were too different for a real friendship to develop, but in many ways he was a publisher's dream: able to write on almost everything, always in the news for one reason or another, so often really memorable. How I wish he had lived longer and been able to give us more!

Yet his was an intensely personal contribution, and because he was also such a complicated man, with such a complicated agenda, he wasn't at all the material of which revolutions are made. He exploded his bomb, saw pieces flying everywhere – and then, instead of advancing, gently sidestepped into something else. *Honest to God* was published in March 1963; in October of the same year he was lecturing in Liverpool – on ethics. His message coincided with another which was to come from Liverpool, sent by the Beatles, who were also rising to fame in 1963: 'All you need is love'.

And there was another controversy – 'the New Morality'.

Of course his next book was eagerly expected, and in March 1965 it appeared. But it wasn't a sequel to *Honest to God.* In many respects it was very different. It was called *The New Reformation?* He was always quite insistent on the question mark. Even then, though, it was fairly clear that the answer to the question in the title was going to be 'no', and that a wider public just wasn't interested in reformations. Part of John Robinson felt that, as is evident from this remarkable prophetic passage.

> Speaking simply from within the situation one knows in England, I become increasingly convinced that the flags of dawn are likely to appear only out of a night a good deal darker yet. For it is not only academic theology which has been living on its own fat. The supply of fat is running out also for the church. It will be a night in which the presuppositions of Christendom, of a traditional power-backed Establishment, are likely to vanish at an accelerating pace. The politeness, the respect, the goodwill on which the church as an institution has been able to presume – and from which it has sought to impose the terms of the debate, culturally and morally – are visibly dissolving. The fat, represented still, for instance, by the inflated figures for infant baptism, could easily be cut by fifty per cent in a generation. Christenings could quickly go the way of 'churchings', which when I was ordained twenty years ago were still part of the religious ethos of working-class England. Compulsory religion in schools will scarcely survive the next major reform, and there is no reason to suppose that religious broadcasting will for ever enjoy its protected 'slot'.[1]

Not bad for 1964!

One reason why John Robinson couldn't be the focus for a lasting revolution was that he never kept still – physically as well as mentally. The fact that this new book, and his next, *Exploration into God*, grew out of lectures in the very different setting of the United States of America, to which he was now constantly being invited, didn't help. And then there was that complex personality.

A look at two words which dominate *Honest to God*, 'honest' and 'radical', is very illuminating here.

People nicknamed him 'Honest John', and the thousands who wrote to him, thanked him for being honest and responded by coming clean themselves. But 'honest' is a more difficult term than it seems at first sight. For example, if I say 'I'm being honest with you,' I may really think that I'm being honest, but others may feel that I haven't really been honest enough *for them*. My upbringing, temperament and training may produce hidden built-in assumptions and blind spots which may cause problems for others, especially if what I say is taken out of context. And that's what happened. John Robinson's 'honesty' in asking radical questions was bound up with another, more hidden, agenda which contained some very conservative items indeed.

This was brilliantly disguised by his interpretation of the word 'radical'. In accepted usage 'radical' is really equivalent to 'thorough', 'sweeping', 'deep', 'far-reaching': we talk of a 'radical' reshuffle, a 'radical' rethink, a 'radical' departure – and by it mean a lot of change. But John Robinson always related 'radical' to its derivation, 'going to the roots', and his roots were thoroughly clerical, Anglican and quite conservatively biblical.

> Being a radical means being an 'insider', an insider to the Sabbath – as Jesus was. The revolutionary can be an 'outsider' to the structure he would see collapse: indeed, he must set himself outside it. But the radical goes to the roots of *his own* tradition. He must love it: he must weep over Jerusalem, even if he has to pronounce its doom. He must believe that the Sabbath really is valuable for man.
>
> This means that the radical must be a man of roots. The revolutionary may be *déraciné*, but not the radical. And that is partly why in our rootless world there are so few genuine radicals. Reformism, too, requires of necessity no depth of root, merely a feel for tradition: hence it can continue to flourish where men have lost their integrity. If the Establishment can thereby be preserved, it may be expedient that

one man should die for the people. For man, after all, is made for the Sabbath.

The roots of the radical, moreover, must go deep enough to provide the security from which to question, even to the fundamentals. No one can be a radical who is uncertain of his tenure – intellectually, morally, or culturally. Only the man who knows he cannot lose what the Sabbath stands for can afford to criticize it radically. Faith alone can dare to doubt – to the depths.

For the same reason a radical is necessarily a man of passion. He is jealous for the truth, the root-meaning, of what the institution has corrupted. He cannot be content to snipe from the sidelines. To be a radical means involvement, commitment. True, it means travelling light, being prepared to laugh at the institution one loves. And therefore he welcomes genuine satire and enjoys seeing the Establishment taken off. For irony is very near to faith – as it was for the Old Testament prophets. But always underneath there is a certain intensity and controlled fire. He has the salt of good humour – but the salt that savours and stings.

The radical is an 'insider' – yet always a bad party-member, an unsafe churchman. He is continually questioning the shibboleths, re-examining the orthodoxies. And he will have a disconcerting habit of finding himself closer to those whose integrity he respects than to those whose conclusions he shares.[2]

This caused considerable confusion, not least in his books. People found them 'muddled' because the arguments were so convoluted and didn't arrive where they seemed to be leading. And John Robinson himself was an almost impossible discussion partner because he didn't seem to want to rule anything out. I remember going to a conference on what had now become 'The New Theology', a year or so after *Honest to God*. Here were those hopefuls who felt that they might be at the dawn of a new beginning in Christian thought and practice, and here too were the professionals, keen to press the author of *Honest to God* on those points where they felt he was evasive, inconsistent or even self-contradictory.

The disappointment of the hopefuls was manifest, when they discovered, on meeting John Robinson face to face, that in temperament he really was an Anglican bishop and was in no way prepared to abandon his rather old-fashioned biblical theology despite the penetrating questions he was asking. And the frustration of the professionals was evident as to every question he replied, 'I think that we must remain open on that point.' Finally, an exasperated philosopher stood up and remarked, 'I would like to remind the Bishop that a vessel which is open on all sides is incapable of containing anything.'

Part of the trouble was that John Robinson didn't actually go to the roots on many issues: he drew on his own, and that's a different matter. Look at the footnotes of his books and you will see the vast amount of literature cited which had only just been published, or which he had picked up in America and hadn't even appeared in Britain yet. Far from being 'radical' in his sense, on closer inspection much of his writing proves to be superficial, and it was only his ability to put his finger on important issues and his journalistic brilliance which carried it off. This superficiality, combined with a refusal to contemplate any kind of programme, proved fatal in the end. *Honest to God* begins and ends with his favourite image of letting everything go into the melting. But in general it seemed that the temperature of the furnace wasn't quite high enough for the process to work properly. And it proved that some things were to be kept out at all costs which many of his readers would have wanted to put in: the Bible, on which he was as conservative as a Conservative Evangelical; the doctrine of the Trinity; and most notably the doctrine of the incarnation (which came to the forefront with the next, more focussed, theological controversy over the *Myth of God Incarnate*). Here he could be almost conventionally sermonic:

> I would want strongly to retain and insist upon the category of 'incarnation'. For in this man, the Christian gospel dares to assert, we see the Word, the Logos, the self-expressive activity of God in all nature and history, what God was and is, enmanned as far as human nature can contain it in an actual historical individual who is bone of our bone, flesh of our flesh – the only truly normal son of man and son of God.

> And I would equally want to insist, strongly, with the New Testament witness that '*God* was in Christ reconciling the world to himself'. In Christ God was doing something for us that we could never do for ourselves. That is the emphasis that those on the inside of Christian theological discourse want to hold to who would cling to substitutionary language, though I would prefer with the great weight of the New Testament witness to stress the *hyper*, on behalf of, rather than the *anti*, instead of; for Christ died not in order that we should not have to die, but precisely so that we could die, to sin rather than because of sin. He died as our representative, not our replacement. And he could do this only as a man who was totally and utterly one of us. Yet his act was God's act.[3]

For me, the give-away in that quotation is the phrase 'those on the inside of Christian theological discourse'. One could also add 'those on the inside of the church'. I don't think it too harsh to say that essentially John Robinson was an insider, flirting with the idea of being an outsider, but not an outsider by temperament – and certainly never interested in making a move in that direction.

But what if you live essentially outside the institution, which is what I do as a publisher? What if most of the time you're immersed in, work in, the secular world just as yourself? In other words, what if you're an ordinary person? Then a lot of things look and feel very different. If you're in search of a faith to live by you can assume less and less, have to question more and more – and somehow find a way through the questions, because no one can live a life worth living on questions alone. That amounts to looking for something beyond a passive liberalism, hoping for some real and substantial change, and realizing that any change is going to demand some effort.

I've found that many people with whom I've talked or corresponded share that kind of feeling, and long for a real focal point. Sadly, that is what *Honest to God* couldn't provide. I'm not at all clear whether John Robinson really wanted the revolution that so many of his eager readers and followers were looking forward to. Certainly he was no revolutionary leader.

It's striking how often his books suggest that things *may* happen (rather than being made to happen), and in the end how little did. A favourite saying of David Jenkins, the present Bishop of Durham, which dates from that time, ran: 'The Church of England is all in favour of change as long as it doesn't make any difference.' That was the trouble with the whole episode.

In the past thirty years there has been no revolution, nor even a real reformation of the kind that John Robinson envisaged. There hasn't even been a comparable theological controversy. In 1977, a dramatic press conference for *The Myth of God Incarnate*, and the involvement of theologians like Don Cupitt, led to substantial media coverage, but it wasn't in the same league. And the book sold a tiny fraction of the copies sold of *Honest to God*. Nor is it easy to see how and where a truly major *theological* controversy could arise in the future. The dominant controversial theologies today, liberation theology and feminist theology, have so far been more about power than about the question of truth, and neither has appealed widely outside the churches.

So what about 'honesty to God' today? Is that no longer an issue? I think it is. There are clearly still many people who feel that the church is not being honest. When there was a furore in the 1980s over the Bishop of Durham's questioning statements on the virgin birth and the resurrection, like John Robinson, he too received thousands of letters of thanks and support for being honest and saying what he believed.

An increasing number of them will have come from outside rather than inside the churches. John Robinson was already drawing attention to the decline in church membership, and in the last thirty years that decline has been even more dramatic in the major denominations in the Western world. The drop would be even more manifest were it not disguised in statistics by a substantial increase in traditions like the evangelical and Pentecostal which are temperamentally and structurally not disposed to questioning.

That has led to polarization and real problems for those who don't want to leave the churches but cannot accept them as they are. I haven't been able to forget a comment made by the

Cambridge theologian Don Cupitt in a conversation a while ago. Men and women training for ministry in the church would come and ask for his understanding: they accepted his radical, non-realist views, which were helpful to them in finding a faith to live by; but they feared that if they stated them openly, it might jeopardize their future in the church. So they were going to play safe, and keep their heads down.

In theological terms, there is no doubt that intellectually the more radical approaches have won the day. The clearest evidence of that is that there are virtually no new substantial and intellectually attractive statements of traditional Christian belief which counter successfully the now well-established criticisms of it. But equally, it is proving virtually impossible for new insights to make their way. What we seem to have is either apathy or deliberate disregard of the many unanswered questions about Christianity, with little attempt to push through them and face the consequences. It's as though *Honest to God* and the far deeper questionings written before or after just didn't exist.

That won't do. For it's abundantly clear that there is no way of putting together the pieces in which Christianity now is so that they add up to the old answers in some miraculously new form, and can provide justification for the churches as they are today. That is why, to take one example, I feel ambivalent about the result of the great campaign in the Church of England for the ordination of women to the priesthood. I'm delighted at its success. But wasn't it, too, more about *power* than anything else? I would be happier had there been more attention to a question in the *Honest to God* tradition which John Robinson touched on but never clearly faced. What *is* priesthood? How can it be defined and practised, if at all, in a secular society without giving the impression that it belongs to a totally different world? This is where closer examination would show that the real issues have still to be tackled. And there are plenty of other areas.

Many people are still prepared to be interested in fundamental questions like the existence of God, the person of Jesus of Nazareth, the basis of morality, not to mention the very nature of language and all the issues raised by 'post-modernism'. But are the churches? There is little evidence that they are. All the signs are that they are concerned above all with the routine of 'business as usual', 'proclaiming the Gospel', being the churches as they have been.

But on what basis? No one would deny the need for their activities in areas of social, pastoral, national and international concern, but that is not the prime *raison d'être* of the churches. Their credentials are a belief which must be put over, lived out and *shown to be true* in dialogue with the outside world. All down history they have been engaged in that dialogue in the intellectual and cultural situation of their time. What happens if they give it up now, as so clearly seems to be happening? Without a coherent intellectual foundation, what defence is there to the charge that much Christian teaching is brainwashing and indoctrination and that in ethos Christianity has become just one more ideology – a closed society run along lines laid down by those who choose to belong to it?

The problems have proved far greater than John Robinson ever envisaged, but at least he was on the right track. That is why, for me, *Honest to God*, warts and all, is something which shouldn't be forgotten. The quest for truth and integrity within the churches, both individual and corporate, still needs to be carried on, even if there is no knowing where it will lead.

Music has always helped me where words give out, and for a long time I have associated Wagner's Ring cycle and its quest for something beyond accepted assumptions and patterns with the questions we've been considering, not least how to change an established order. At a pivotal point in the drama Wotan remarks to Fricka, the symbol of that order, 'Your concern is only for what we are used to; I'm looking for something which has yet to happen.' The something involves the twilight of the gods and the fall of Valhalla, but beyond that there is the new. I, too, am looking for that, but the night is pretty dark. Still, I keep hoping.

The Aweful Truth: Thoughts on the Last Things

Ruth Etchells

One of our most popular singers has dreamed of it. 'Everyone,' he says, 'everyone's gonna have a wonderful time up there ...' Have *you* thought about Heaven recently? Or the other place, if it comes to that? As a child I used to be much troubled about hell; and I'd read with anxious care all the bits of the Bible that tell you who goes there. As the hero of *Three Men in a Boat* found when reading the medical dictionary, I seemed to have every symptom of impending disaster it described. But what do *you* really think we're heading for, each of us, when this life's done? And what do you truly think will happen eventually to 'the world, the universe, and everything ...'? The 'last things', in fact; for you personally, for those you love, and for history?

It's a question that different theologians have offered very different views on. John Robinson was one of the most controversial. I have his book, *Honest to God*, in front of me now; rather tatty and grubby, and written all over, often quite fiercely, in my handwriting of thirty years ago.

My handwriting has changed quite a lot in these thirty years, and so have some of my reactions. I'm now able to honour his intention because he wanted to share with people a way of thinking about God he'd found liberating. The problem he'd faced was that a twentieth-century space-age could surely no longer go for a 'mysterious God', in a three-decker universe of Hell below, Earth in the middle, and Heaven above. So, he said, the picture-language must go, of God-up-there far above the starry skies. The first satellite in space, Sputnik, had been launched in 1957, six years before *Honest to God* was published.

And from then on there was hardware in the heavens. So the mystery of 'beyond the skies' now seemed to be all about – not God – but how far *human beings* could go. So John Robinson believed that what one might call the supernatural paraphernalia of Heaven was getting in the way of our grappling with the *real* wonder and truth and grace of God. That, for him, was the point: how to hold on to that reality of God when the picture language failed. And that's what I can honour in his writing now – the urgency with which he fought to find a way to talk about God which would convey God's reality for twentieth-century people. So, since 'up there', and 'out there' language hadn't any reality for us (he believed) we must look, instead, 'in here': within ourselves, in everyday relationships.

For that's where we'd find Jesus 'the man for others': where we do our hard daily living. As George Herbert put it, long ago, 'Teach me, my God and King, In all things Thee to see' ... How we respond to Tom, Dick and Harry in the sort of selfless way that puts them first and our instinct to please ourselves last, making Christ's crucifixion the basis of our lives: that, for John Robinson, was true and real God-talk. For him, that's where we find the deepest reality in which everything is grounded, the reality which is the God who is Love. Not in a so-called 'holy place', and not in some mysterious other-dimension called 'Heaven'.

Well, re-reading all that, thirty years on, I was moved and touched and even challenged by the sharp reminder that wherever else we look for God, he *must* be found by us in the coin of daily exchange, in how we are with other people. Without that, any other kind of Heaven is mere escapism. That was a truth as powerful – and as biblical – when I re-read it last week, as it was when John Robinson so strongly insisted on it in 1963. And I found it made me look again at whether I do truly seek God myself in my own network of relationships, and how far I'm prepared to deny myself and share Christ's cross in them. That's quite a Lenten exercise: certainly for me it has become a penitential one.

And yet; the Heaven the Bible describes, the Heaven Christ promised us, is a lot more glorious and victorious than that. And so, the more I re-read the book, the more I found myself boxed in by narrowness in its vision: it was so fundamentally human-centred, and the truth about creation and its Creator is vaster than that. And the book wobbled between two viewpoints, as we shall see. And it made sweeping and dismissive assumptions.

For instance, take those assumptions from which the book began. That the language of 'the holy', of immeasurable transcendence beyond our very imagining, was not compatible with space travel and modern philosophy, where, it seemed, all mystery would eventually be wholly explicable ... So the thinking ran.

Yet: in 1968, only a year before the first moon landing finally took place in 1969, in front of a world glued to its telly, there was a space flight right round the moon – ten times round it, actually, before coming back to earth. And the climax of that flight was on Christmas Day, 1968, when Colonel Frank Borman, astronaut commander, read from space the opening verses of the Book of Genesis. Five years *after* the publication of *Honest to God.* So I guess I wasn't alone – though it felt like it – when in 1963 I wrote across the pages of that little blue book that God's mystery, and the nature of Heaven, were no more reducible to measurement by Sputnik and the human intelligence that produced it, than they had been measurable by the Tower of Babel and the human intelligence which built that. And that some theologians would do well to muse on this. For like those who built Babel, in the story, they seemed to want to reduce everything to the littleness of human understanding ...

And that's where I still take issue most passionately with John Robinson's version of Heaven. For he threw out for many people what the pictures were always only a glimpse of anyway: the truth that by definition God is always 'beyond' us – wherever in space or depth psychology or robotic technology we get to: *beyondness is a pre-requisite of God.* And today there is a great hunger that this should be recognized. 'Honesty' today means we give transcendence its place. We still need to look for God where we live, but the God we hope to find must be holy as well as intimate, not tame, user-friendly and domesticated.

Beethoven had on his desk words that he had written out and framed, that put it exactly:

I, God, am that which is.
I am all that is, that was and that shall be.
No mortal man hath lifted my veil.

God is alone by Himself, and to Him alone
do all things own their being.

Now, this is where John Robinson 'wobbled': because although much of the book was apparently exactly opposite to ideas of the God who is 'beyond', every now and again he seemed to take fright. When he did, he would then talk in quite a different way. For instance, in a memorable passage in *Honest to God* he wrote:

> There are depths of revelation, intimations of eternity, judgments of the holy and the sacred, awarenesses of the unconditional, the numinous and the ecstatic, which cannot be explained in purely naturalistic categories without being reduced to something else.[1]

But then he would swing back, and reduce God to the God within, not a God who was beyond as well. And I think that the reason he wobbled between these two visions of God, rather than seeing them as one whole, was because he concentrated almost entirely on the *crucified* Christ, and left out the Easter Christ, the risen Lord. The 'mysterious bit', in fact.

For yes, indeed, taking into all our daily dealings with others the power of the crucifixion – this is the stuff of eternal life. *But it is so only because there was a resurrection as well as a crucifixion.* Resurrection – a raising up again by the mysterious power of God – as well as a crucifixion – a spreadeagled corpse, killed for other people. And it was – and is – John Robinson's failure in *Honest to God* to give the resurrection its place in the Good News, that I find, still, so diminishing to his message.

For whatever lies beyond death for us, whatever lies in the mystery of eternity for this world and all that it inhabits, is safeguarded for us by the Easter Christ's overcoming of all the Good Friday Christ suffered.

Although much of the biblical account of all this has to be

picture language to describe the indescribable, nevertheless we must recognize it is something *real* that is being described: a picture, a metaphor, to describe a real event, a *real* power. It changed and changes lives. As Norman Nicholson once wrote, about the picture language of Moses seeing the burning bush:

When Moses, musing in the desert, found
The thorn bush spiking up from the hot ground,
And saw the branches, on a sudden, bear
The crackling yellow barberries of fire,

He searched his learning and imagination
For any logical, neat explanation,
And turned to go, but turned again and stayed,
And faced the fire and knew it for his God.

I too have seen the briar alight like coal,
The love that burns, the flesh that's ever whole,
And many times have turned and left it there,
Saying: 'It's prophecy – but metaphor'.

But stinging tongues like John the Baptist shout:
'That this is metaphor is no way out.
It's dogma too, or you make God a liar;
The bush is still a bush, and fire is fire.'[2]

Indeed it was the truth that these two facts were of *equal* reality, Christ's dying and his rising, which the earliest theologians were so careful to insist on. Take St Paul:

> For what I received I passed on to you as of first importance: that Christ died for our sins according to the scriptures, that he was buried, that he was raised on the third day according to the scriptures, and that he appeared, ... he appeared, ... he appeared, ... he appeared.... And if Christ has not been raised, our preaching is useless and so is your faith. If for this life only we have hope in Christ, we are to be pitied more than all men. But Christ has indeed been raised from the dead, the first fruits of those who have fallen asleep. For since

death came through a man, the resurrection of the dead comes also through a man. For as in Adam all die, so in Christ all will be made alive ... Listen, I tell you a mystery ... The perishable must clothe itself with the imperishable, and the mortal with immortality (I Cor. 15.3–8, 51, 53).

As the anthem 'This joyful Eastertide' puts it:

Had Christ, that once was slain,
  Ne'er burst his three-days prison,
Our faith had been in vain;
  But now hath Christ arisen,
  Arisen, arisen, arisen![3]

So, in contradiction of *Honest to God*, I'd want to urge the transcendent 'beyondness' of God as a wonder and a delight, not at all as an intolerable burden to belief. What awaits us after death and how it joins on to what we have been and known during our life on earth – all this is part of that 'beyondness'.

To take up the two questions which John Robinson rightly insisted in *Honest to God* were important ones: Does this say anything to how we live now? And what sort of future does it offer, beyond this time and this place? When I was angry with John Robinson and some of his mentors, like the theologian Paul Tillich, it was because much of what they said led many to believe there was nothing beyond physical death, to feel cut off from the hope of Heaven.

And there are consequences for this present life. For a people trapped by that kind of no hope can easily become prey to the sort of evil that follows mortal despair. So I was fascinated to find, in one of those moments when John Robinson was wobbling in his argument, that he quoted from Tillich words which actually conceded this very point:

> Our period has decided for a *secular* world. That was a great and much-needed decision ... It gave consecration and holiness to our daily life and work. Yet it excluded those

> things for which religion stands: the feeling for the inexhaustible mystery of life, the grip of an ultimate meaning of existence, and the invincible power of an inexhaustible devotion. These things *cannot* be excluded. If we try to expel them in their divine images, they re-emerge in daemonic images. Now, in the old age of our secular world, we have seen the most horrible manifestations of these daemonic images; we have looked more deeply into the mystery of evil than most generations before us; we have seen the unconditional devotion of millions to a satanic image; we feel our period's sickness unto death.[4]

That was written in the aftermath of World War II, with its sickening discoveries of the Hitler death camps. What both Tillich and John Robinson were conceding was that *we disregard the judgments of eternity at our peril.* Yet how do we talk of these judgments?

One of the Bible pictures that tended to get thrown out, along with all the other Heaven language, was the picture of a Judgment Day, a sort of Heavenly Assize Court. Thrown out not least because 'honesty' in John Robinson's time quite rightly involved recognizing that this picture meant absolutely nothing to most people.

Yet our Christian forefathers who lived in expectation of such a 'Heavenly Assize' lived in some fear of it, but also in great hope. Because they wanted to see evil – not petty or trivial misdemeanour, but the kind of evil that can destroy people – they wanted to see that kind of evil publicly shown as defeated. Inspector Morse, in an episode recently re-shown, said of someone who had given drugs to children and then been killed in a police car chase, 'I don't believe in Hell; but for folk like him, I wish I did.'

For that biblical picture was a vivid image of one necessity of the eternity of Heaven: that amongst its qualities must be 'justice'.

Well, that image may not work any better for many people now than it did back in John Robinson's time. But perhaps the honesty of our times is leading us to seek more urgently the truth, mysterious as it is, that it was about. Perhaps it is time to re-discover the marvellous truth that we do not face the vastness of eternity alone and uncared for, or at the disposal of a vengeful God; but shielded by a Love as wide as eternity, and as generous, a God whose profound care is our welfare and whose face is known to us in one called Jesus.

O more and more Thy love extend,
My life befriend with heavenly pleasure;
That I may win Thy paradise,
Thy pearl of price, thy countless treasure;
Since but in Thee I can go free
From earthly care and vain oppression,
This prayer I make for Jesus sake,
That Thou me take in Thy possession.[5]

Because at some point we turned the picture of the 'Heavenly Assize' into a message almost entirely of punishment and exile, we lost the essential meaning of that picture: that the God 'beyond', by his very nature wills to 'set things right', and that this is what the Bible means by 'judgment'. However else John Robinson and I differ theologically, I'm sure we'd have agreed on that.

The poet James Stephens has a dream about the kindness of God's justice in the fullness of time:

On a rusty iron throne
Past the furthest star of space
I saw Satan sit alone,
Old and haggard was his face;
For his work was done and he
Rested in eternity.

And to him from out the sun
Came his father and his friend
Saying, now the work is done
Enmity is at an end:
And he guided Satan to
Paradises that he knew.

Gabriel without a frown,
Uriel without a spear,
Raphael came singing down
Welcoming their ancient peer,
And they seated him beside
One who had been crucified.[6]

How God will, at some point beyond our vision, enable us to see for ourselves the reality of wholly effective justice combined with total and most compassionate mercy as the way things really are, this is the ultimate mystery. But we have been given reassurances about it throughout our history.

The 'honesty' of *Honest to God* meant cutting out the language of 'up there' and 'out there'. 'Honesty' for us today has a different challenge: how to hold on to the 'things beyond' as real and precious, by finding a language for them that conveys the 'beyondness', and yet is of our own time. One of the writers who has best done this for us in the second half of the twentieth century is the novelist William Golding, for instance in his book, *The Paper Men*. The main character, who is a novelist, is in flight from a man who wants to be his official biographer, and who is, therefore, an image of the Recording Angel facing one at Judgment Day, at the Heavenly Assize. He flees from country to country: and on some remote Greek island he finds in a cathedral a terrifying statue of Christ. It's like a vision of God the Terrible Judge.

> I stood there with my mouth open and the flesh crawling over my body. I knew in one destroying instant that all my life I had believed in God and this knowledge was a vision of God. Fright entered the very marrow of my bones ... Adrift in the universal intolerance, mouth open, screaming ... I knew my maker and I fell down.[7]

It's like all those terrible mediaeval paintings we have seen of the damned falling towards hell, 'adrift in the universal intolerance', with mouths open, screaming. The doctor says it was 'a stroke'. He knows a deeper truth. Convalescent in Rome, he struggles to come to terms with it. He has realized, as he says, 'what a mess I must be'. One day he has gone up to his balcony and put his head between his hands and tried to think, when suddenly he becomes certain that God is standing on top of the church opposite: 'he could simply step across from the roof and collect me', he says. He's dazed with terror: and it's then he has a kind of dream. He thought he was standing on the church roof with God, looking down at its steps:

> There was sunlight everywhere, not the heavy light of Rome but a kind of radiance as if the sun were everywhere ... I saw that the steps had the symmetrical curve of a musical instrument, guitar, cello, violin. But this harmonious shape was now embellished and interrupted by the people and the flowers and the litter of jewels strewn among them on the steps. All the people were young and like flowers ... (God) was standing by me ... and we went down together and stood among the people with the pattern of jewels and the heaps of flowers all blazing inside and out with the radiance. Then ... they held hands and moved and the movement was music. I saw they were neither male nor female or perhaps they were both and it was of no importance. What mattered was the music they made ...
>
> There were steps going down, narrow steps to a door with a sea beyond it ... Also there were creatures in the sea that sang. For the singing and the song I have no words at all.[8]

Judgment transmuted by Grace. That is the aweful truth: the eternal human destiny we are all called to, in this life, but also beyond this life. I'm glad I was asked to look again at *Honest to God*. For thirty years on, it's helped me to get quite clear what honesty demands today: and to ponder thankfully on the transcendent God in whom we may, afresh, honestly believe.

Truth is Many-Eyed

Alan Race

Honesty means to tell the truth about what you see. Looking at the religious landscape of Britain, I see a society of many religions – Buddhists, Jews, Hindus, Muslims, Baha'is, Jains, Sikhs, Christians. A multi-faith society of living religions. We used to think that religions other than Christianity belonged to far away, exotic or strange places. Today, there is nothing unusual about meeting people with different religious traditions in our everyday lives, in our neighbourhood, at work, or at leisure.

What does honesty mean in the face of this supermarket of religious possibilities? First of all, it means knowing that in Britain, a minority of about five per cent of the population belong to religious traditions other than the Christian faith, a figure roughly comparable with the percentage of practising Christians in the population as a whole. When it comes to attendance at religious rituals, there may be little difference between those who go to a Christian church, and those who attend at the Muslim mosque, the Sikh gurdwara, the Jewish synagogue.

Rarely is honesty a comforting word. In fact, I find it is a tough, disturbing word, once we begin to tell the truth about what we see. For me, this disturbing experience of the supermarket of religions is portrayed well by the Jewish writer, Chaim Potok, in a novel entitled *The Book of Lights*. In this novel, Gershon is a Jewish chaplain in the army. He is sent to the Far East, and visits Japan. One day, in a busy street, he comes across a shrine from the Japanese religion of Shinto. His eye is caught by an old man praying, surrounded by candles and stood before an altar. Gershon asks his friend, John, what he makes of it all:

> 'Do you think our God is listening to him, John?'
>
> 'I don't know, chappy. I never thought of it.'
>
> 'Neither did I until now. If He's not listening, why not? If He is listening, then – well, what are *we* all about, John?'[1]

'What are *we* all about?' I meet faithfulness in an unfamiliar guise, and the experience forces me to ask questions of honesty about my own religious conviction. Is there only 'one valid vision' of truth before God? Or does my religious conviction owe as much to where I was born as it does to the inspiration I find in it?

When John Robinson wrote his book *Honest to God* in 1963, he disturbed many people by suggesting that we need to rethink our image of God, for the sake of credibility in the modern world. Now once we admit that this is a task in which all religions share, the search for honesty can unsettle us even more. John Robinson himself knew this when he received an invitation in the mid 1970s to give some lectures in India: '... one would be compelled,' he said, 'to look at truth through a different glass of vision. And this was disturbing if not threatening.' In the event, Robinson found the trip to India to be a real invigoration for his own faith. The encounter with another religious culture may induce fear. But as John Robinson's example showed, it is more likely to turn out to be a surprise for the good.

When the mediaeval Catholic Church thought of the world they thought of their European boundaries. And within those boundaries, it seemed natural that the Christian view of God reigned supreme. Jews could be vilified as Christ-killers, and Muslims dismissed as infidels. With the invention of global travel, the journeys to the Americas and the Far East, the question of God's presence among other, unknown peoples sparked off a deeper debate about what God has been up to *beyond* the borders of Europe. The traditional answer that 'there is no salvation outside the church' began to seem a little threadbare. Today, it strikes many of us as rather small-minded, and a shade imperialistic. As the world struggles towards becoming a global community, where many faiths have a place in the sun, there is a challenge about how to picture God's presence in the world honestly, that has not been faced in quite this way before.

You do not need to go to another country to encounter people of another religious culture. In Britain, we can now share the experience of different faith-traditions through visiting the places of devotion of our Buddhist or Baha'i friends, or through working together on common causes to build a more just society. Let me give you some examples of both of these experiences.

Whenever I enter a place of devotion of another faith, I am aware of stepping into what seems like another religious universe. Visit the Jain temple in Leicester – the biggest in Europe, or the Buddhist monastery in Sussex, or the Central Mosque in Regent's Park: for me as a Christian, the strangeness can be overwhelming. Yet there is also a beauty of spirit in these sacred spaces, and I yield to its attractiveness.

Strangeness and attraction – a double movement of the heart. Religious honesty compels me to hold on to both of these feelings. Here are some examples of spiritual flowering, from three traditions – they illustrate that double movement of the heart I have in mind.

First, in this extract from the Buddhist scriptures:

> The Blessed One said: 'Whatever grounds there be for good works done in this world, all of them are not worth one-sixteenth part of that love which is the heart's release. Love alone, which is the heart's release, shines and burns and flashes forth in surpassing them.[2]

Secondly, from the ancient prayer of the Jews, the Kaddish:

> Glorified and sanctified be God's great name throughout the world which He has created according to His will. May He establish his kingdom in your lifetime and during your days,

and within the life of the entire house of Israel, speedily and soon, and say, Amen.'

Finally, listen to this poem, calling down love in prayer, inspired by the Hindu Vedantic tradition:

> Not for me is the love that knows no restraint, but like the foaming wine that, having burst its vessel in a moment, would run to waste.
>
> Send me the love which is cool and pure, like your rain that blesses the thirsty earth and fills the homely earthen jars.
>
> Send me the love that would soak down into the centre of being, and from there would spread like the unseen sap through the branching tree of life, giving birth to fruits and flowers.
>
> Send me the love that keeps the heart still with the fullness of peace.[3]

That was from the Indian writer, Rabindranath Tagore. I could illustrate this shared festival of the spirit many times over. It cuts across the old religious barriers, and invites anyone to share in its resonance.

There are other ways to overcome the mutual suspicion that religious people have been taught to hold for one another. There is what some Asian Christians have called the 'dialogue of everyday life' – learning trust in our relationships, in neighbourliness, and through all the little human gestures that help to create community. At another level it means working together as citizens for a fairer society. Issues of local justice, housing, racism, education, the law, the environment – these are all concerns around which religious people of differing *belief* convictions are learning to unite. This shared work represents a slow but steady increase in honesty in recent years. For Hindus, Muslims, Sikhs, Jews, and others, have not always felt that they were welcome in Britain, let alone welcome as equal partners with the Christian churches.

To value another's spiritual tradition and to work together for a better society leads me to ask about the vision of God that corresponds to these new historical circumstances. As a Christian priest, I must ask: how honest am I if I restrict my vision of God to what comes through my tradition alone? And honesty begs me to go beyond even tolerance – towards the real theological embrace of a multi-cultural, multi-ethnic and multi-faith society.

As people from different religious traditions learn to trust one another as people of faith, I believe we shall be led to see that all of them are in some sense responding to the same divine reality which animates the world from within our experience. This reality, whom Christians call God, Muslims call Allah, and Hindus name as Brahman. When, in 1979, John Robinson produced his book with the intriguing title *Truth is Two-Eyed*, I was grateful to him for expressing this belief sharply:

> The God who discloses himself in Jesus and the God who discloses himself in Krishna must be the same God, or he is no God – and there is no revelation at all. *Ultimately* for both sides there are not 'gods many and lords many' but one God, under whatever name . . .[4]

Robinson was not proposing here that all religions were really the same underneath their outward cultural appearance. He wanted to be *more* honest than that – honest to the facts of the similarities and the differences between the religions. He thought of those differences as a choice between two types of religion – one he called prophetic religion and the other mystical religion.

This led him to a global religious vision which he pictured as an ellipse – an oval with two centres, one at each end. The centre at one end stood for the cluster of prophetic religions associated with the West – mainly Judaism, Christianity and Islam – and the centre at the other end of the ellipse represented the cluster of mystical religions associated with the East – mainly Hinduism and Buddhism. This was a rough picture, but it had the advantage of showing how two types of religion can exist in a state of mutual belonging without becoming all mixed up.

The churches, at the official level, have not really been able to endorse this bold move in theological imagination. It seems to surrender too much of the traditional supremacy of the Christian religion. Moreover, it threatens to undermine the unique position of the central Christian reality, the person of Jesus Christ. And what about Christian mission? These questions represent real anxieties. But I think that they are born out of a misplaced fear. The traditional Christian claim to supremacy was often founded on the theological principle that Christian faith was a revealed religion, and other religions were human inventions. But, in the light of the spiritual depth and quality of moral life that all the ancient living religions inspire, this argument has ceased to carry conviction. There are no arguments left now to support the supremacy of Christianity except those born of sheer prejudice.

This may be a hard lesson for some Christians to learn, but to pretend otherwise is like trying to close the stable door after the horse has bolted. Of course, the implications of these developments reach deep down into the Christian psyche – and that is the reason for the anxieties.

For example, there will be some far-reaching adjustments in belief to make. Christians will need to learn commitment to the Jesus-shaped view of God without the dogmatism or the absolutism of the past, and without the judgmentalism of the past. Yet the central commitment – that God has become known to the world through Jesus – remains in place. The difference now is that there is no reason at all why Christians should think that this commitment automatically entails the redundancy of every other tried and tested religious pathway. We require a more modest tone. Less of the strident triumphalism, and more of the mutual listening.

The same will also be true, of course, for disciples from other religious communities. If the world is like a house, and the religions occupy different rooms in the house, then we cannot continue to think that one room is special above the other rooms. However, there may be something special, yet very different, to be found in all the rooms.

Most of the churches are now moving towards the acceptance of some degree of truth in other religious traditions. There has been a cautious growth in dialogue as a way of moving forward together in mutual respect, each religion realizing that the truth is bigger than they once thought. But honesty in dialogue could not only heal our caution, but also yield a surprise of its own. For dialogue implies that each religion has its own validity before the truth. Truth, after all, is not one-eyed, perhaps not even two-eyed, but may turn out to be many-eyed.

There is a uniqueness at the heart of every ancient living religion. For Christians, this uniqueness will be found in the face of Jesus. And John Robinson himself was keen to stress this. For others, the divine reality will radiate to the world through a different lens. The reality of our multi-faith society requires that Christians and others come to terms with different visions of religious truth.

One of my favourite passages about honesty in a multi-faith world comes from a former General Secretary of the Church Missionary Society, Max Warren, writing, in fact, four years before *Honest to God*, in 1959:

> Our first task in approaching another people, another culture, another religion, is to take off our shoes, for the place we are approaching is holy. Else we may find ourselves treading on men's dreams. More serious still, we may forget that God was here before our arrival.[5]

Perhaps this is the most basic honesty that the religions should strive for. It undermines their competitive clamour, and urges humility.

Honesty takes us to the threshold of the unfamiliar. To meet another religious culture is simply to meet the divine reality in an unfamiliar form. And the divine reality, whom Christians call God, always sees differently from us. Therefore God's blessing to us is that the search for honesty is a never-ending quest. 'We may forget that God was here before our arrival.' I hope not.

Notes

The Flowering of Honesty
Eric James

The music accompanying this broadcast was taken from
Bach, *The Well-Tempered Clavier*, Book I: Prelude No. XXI in B flat; Book II: Fugue No. XXII in B flat minor, Prelude No. XII in F minor and Prelude No. VIII in E flat minor.

1. Philip Larkin, 'Annus Mirabilis' from *High Windows*, Faber & Faber 1974. Reprinted by permission.
2. Extract from an article by John A. T. Robinson published in the *Sunday Mirror*, 7 April 1963, and reprinted by permission. See pp. 11–13 of this book for the full text.
3. John A. T. Robinson, *Christian Morals Today*, SCM Press 1964, pp. 9, 10, 11, 33. Reprinted in *Christian Freedom in a Permissive Society*, SCM Press 1970.
4. From an article entitled 'Probes at Woolwich' by F. C. Coppleston, published in *The Month*, July 1965. Reprinted by permission of the Editor.
5. John A. T. Robinson, *Exploration into God*, SCM Press 1967, p. 15.
6. John A. T. Robinson, 'Learning from Cancer' in *Where Three Ways Meet: Last Essays and Sermons*, SCM Press 1987, pp. 189–194. Also included in Eric James, *A Life of Bishop John A. T. Robinson*, Collins 1987, pp. 304–309.

Life was Never the Same
Ruth Robinson

The music accompanying this broadcast was taken from
Schubert, String Quintet in C, 1st and 2nd movements.

1. From Joanna Trollope, *The Rector's Wife*, Bloomsbury Publishing Ltd 1991. Copyright © Joanna Trollope 1991.

2. Richard Bach, *Illusions: The Adventures of a Reluctant Messiah*, Heinemann 1977, paragraphs 11–20. © Creative Enterprises Inc. 1977.
3. Edward Robinson, *The Language of Mystery*, SCM Press 1987, pp. 29, 40f.
4. *Illuminations of Hildegard Bingen* (1098–1179), Bear & Co., Santa Fé 1985, p. 33.
5. John Steinbeck, *East of Eden*, Heinemann 1968. © John Steinbeck.
6. Kathleen Raine, 'The Presence' from *Poems 1984–87*, Golgonooza Press 1987. Used by permission of the author.
7. Meister Eckhart (1260–1329), German Dominican mystic and prophet, was the greatest spokesman of the creation-centred spiritual tradition.
8. William Blake (1757–1827), 'The Divine Image' from *Songs of Innocence* (1789).
9. Thomas Traherne (1637?–1674), *Centuries of Meditation*, Cent. iii (first published 1908).

A Loss of Nerve
John Bowden

The music used in this broadcast was
The Beatles, 'All you need is love'
The closing moments of Richard Wagner's opera *Götterdämmerung*

1. John A. T. Robinson, *The New Reformation?*, SCM Press 1965, p. 101.
2. John A. T. Robinson, *Christian Freedom in a Permissive Society*, SCM Press 1970, pp. 3–4.
3. John A. T. Robinson, 'What Future for a Unique Christ?' in *Where Three Ways Meet: Last Essays and Sermons*, SCM Press 1987, p. 11.

The Aweful Truth: Thoughts on the Last Things
Ruth Etchells

The music used in this broadcast was
Pat Boone, 'Gospel Boogie'
Mozart, 'Sanctus' from the *Requiem*
Anthem by W. W. Harris, 'Faire is the heaven', recorded by the Vassari Singers, conductor Jeremy Backhouse
'This Joyful Eastertide', recorded by the Cambridge Singers, conductor John Rutter; tune based on a seventeenth-century Dutch melody

'Thee will I love, my God and King', recorded by Durham Cathedral Choir; tune 'Crossings' by Armstrong Gibbs
Walford Davies, 'Requiem', recorded by King's College, Cambridge, conductor David Willcocks, among *The Psalms of David*

1. John A. T. Robinson, *Honest to God*, SCM Press 1963, p. 55.
2. Norman Nicholson, 'The Burning Bush' in *Five Rivers*, Faber & Faber 1944.
3. Refrain of the hymn 'This Joyful Eastertide', words by G. R. Woodward (1848–1934).
4. Paul Tillich, *The Shaking of the Foundations*, SCM Press 1949; Penguin 1962, p. 181. As quoted by Robinson in *Honest to God*, pp. 54ff.
5. Last verse of the hymn 'Thee will I love, my God and King', words by Robert Bridges (1844–1930).
6. James Stephens, 'The Fullness of Time' in *Collected Poems*, Macmillan 1954. Reprinted by permission of Mrs Iris Wise and the Society of Authors as the literary representations of the Estate of James Stephens.
7. William Golding, *The Paper Men*, Faber & Faber 1984, p. 123.
8. Ibid., pp. 160, 161.

Truth is Many-Eyed
Alan Race

The music accompanying this broadcast was
Collecting the Harvest, Egyptian piece, composer unknown
Imran Khan, *Gat – Madhya Jhaptal*, performed on surbahar and sitar by composer
Albert Roussel, *Krishna*
Claude Debussy, *Syrinx*

1. Chaim Potok, *The Book of Lights*, Heinemann 1982.
2. *Itivuttaka*, I.3, 7, Pali Canon.
3. Rabindranath Tagore (1861–1941).
4. John A. T. Robinson, *Truth is Two-Eyed*, SCM Press 1979, p. 98.
5. Part of Max Warren's General Introduction to the 'Christian Presence' series, the first title of which was Kenneth Cragg, *Sandals at the Mosque*, SCM Press 1959.